CALLED TO

Sermons by Salvation Army Women

*This book, an initiative of Commissioner Helen Clifton,
former World President of Women's Ministries,
is dedicated to her memory.
She was promoted to Glory shortly before its publication in 2011.*

Salvation Books
The Salvation Army International Headquarters
London, United Kingdom

Published by Salvation Books
The Salvation Army International Headquarters
101 Queen Victoria Street, London EC4V 4EH, United Kingdom

Printed in the UK by Polestar Wheatons, Exeter

Contents

Page

Foreword General Linda Bond   v

Practical Holiness   1
Major Maureen Ashton *New Zealand, Fiji and Tonga Territory*

A City of Refuge   7
Major Stacy Birks *USA Western Territory*

Choosing to Respond   11
Captain Robyn Black *Australia Eastern Territory*

Standing in the Gap   17
Major Patricia Brown *United Kingdom Territory with the Republic of Ireland*

Mothers with a Message for Today   23
Captain Leanne Browski *Southern Africa Territory*

Make Me a Captive, Lord!   31
Lieut-Colonel Susan Bukiewicz *USA Central Territory*

What is 'Fellowsment'?   37
Major Betzann Carroll *USA Eastern Territory*

Time to Shout   43
Major Sharon Clanfield *Australia Eastern Territory*

Total Freedom   49
Captain Jenny Collings *New Zealand, Fiji and Tonga Territory*

Faith or Forgery?   55
Major Lesa Davis *USA Central Territory*

Broken Dolls Restored   61
Major Marlene George *Canada and Bermuda Territory*

The Healing of the Paralysed Man   67
Major Ronda Gilger *USA Western Territory*

God Does Things Differently   73
Major Bente Gundersen *Rwanda and Burundi Command*

That's My King!   79
Captain Jennifer Hale *Canada and Bermuda Territory*

The People Who Walked in Darkness Have Seen a Great Light   85
Colonel Margaret Hay *New Zealand, Fiji and Tonga Territory*

Get the Rewards You Really Deserve   91
Major Suzanne Hay *New Zealand, Fiji and Tonga Territory*

Faith Under Fire   99
Major Heather Jenkins *Australia Southern Territory*
Trust in God   103
Major Tracey Kasuso *Southern Africa Territory*
Are You a Roof-breaker?   107
Major Paula Knight *Brazil Territory*
The Word of God in Today's World   115
Colonel Naomi Lalngaihawmi *India Eastern Territory*
Forgiveness and Salvation – the Start of a Holy Life   119
Major Karin Larsson *Sweden and Latvia Territory*
Quite Intrusive   125
Colonel Edith Löfgren *Sweden and Latvia Territory*
Calvary Questions   129
Commissioner Gudrun Lydholm *Denmark Territory*
Rescue Me   133
Major Jenine Main *United Kingdom Territory with the Republic of Ireland*
Human Weakness Equals Perfection in God   137
Major Liliana Makagiantang *Indonesia Territory*
Walk of Holiness   141
Captain Wilma L. Mason *USA Southern Territory*
The *I Ams* of John the Baptist   147
Major Elsa Oalang *The Philippines Territory*
To Tell the Truth   153
Major Kelly Pontsler *USA Western Territory*
To Give to God   159
Captain Josephine Sabir Masih *Pakistan Territory*
Our Thoughts are Contrary to Those of God   163
Captain Japhette Sinda *Congo (Brazzaville) Territory*
Make a Garden   167
Major Kathryn Trim *Canada and Bermuda Territory*
Citizens of Heaven   177
Major Marieke Venter *Southern Africa Territory*
Prayer, our Daily Food   183
Major Sabrina Williams *Caribbean Territory*
I Know He Watches Me   187
Major Morag Yoder *USA Central Territory*
Forward with Prayer   195
Lieut-Colonel Rebecca Yousaf *Pakistan Territory*

Foreword

This collection of sermons by Salvationist women preachers is a very important book. It deserves to be read, used and shared, for four good reasons:

- It reflects our strong heritage and shows us that what Catherine Booth won for us in the Army's earliest days, is carried on with quality and clarity. Women have a right to speak and to preach.
- It is a book dedicated to the memory of Commissioner Helen Clifton by whose initiative this project came about. The commissioner had a heart for the gospel and its proclamation by women.
- Perhaps the most important reason is caught in the title, *Called to Preach*. For Salvationists, this goes to the very heart of the matter, before and beyond Catherine Booth and Helen Clifton. The writers and preachers are communicating that they have been obedient to a calling upon their lives. The Lord has appointed them and anointed them to preach. He has something to say to us through these sermons. That is reason enough to read, listen and respond.
- But lastly and significantly, this is an inspiring collection of messages.

I recommend it heartily.

Linda Bond
GENERAL

Major Maureen Ashton
New Zealand, Fiji and Tonga Territory

Practical Holiness

Titus 2:12-13

TO be holy means 'to be set apart for God's holy use'. How do we maintain practical holiness while we wait?

Holiness teaches us to say 'no' to ungodliness and worldly passions, and to live self-controlled, upright and godly lives in this present age, while we wait for the blessed hope – the glorious appearing of our great God and Saviour, Jesus Christ.

In simple terms, holiness is to be set apart. Some things God declared holy sanctified and set apart for his use in the sanctuary. They were objects but we are not, so we don't just sit around being set apart. We need to be vigilant in maintaining ourselves as holy vessels, consecrated and available for God's use at any time.

God is set apart from everything because of his holiness but that doesn't mean he doesn't want to be involved with his creation. He is not a distant God, remote and unfeeling. He actually loves and cares for his creation, even those who choose to take a different road. He expects us as his children to be the same. 'For it is written: "Be holy, because I am holy"' (1 Peter 1:16).

God has set us apart but this does not give us licence to ignore the world. The process of setting ourselves apart for God is a journey and includes making changes, moving forward, applying godly principles to our lives and discarding any ungodly baggage that will weigh us down and hinder our progress.

'Therefore, since we are surrounded by such a great cloud of witnesses, let us throw off everything that hinders and the sin that so easily entangles. And let us run with perseverance the race marked out for us' (Hebrews 12:1).

It's like deciding to take a trip, planning it, knowing where you're heading, packing your provisions and resources and using a map or GPS system to help you get there. Along the way you may discover it necessary to reroute or just pause to enjoy the scenery or to assess the trip so far.

The journey to holiness is the same and we have a map for our use and a guide – it's called the Bible. This is in keeping with the Word in 2 Corinthians 7:1 *KJV* saying, 'Having therefore these promises, dearly beloved, let us cleanse ourselves from all filthiness of the flesh and spirit, perfecting holiness in the fear of God.'

Some people set out on this journey to live the holy life by trying to make themselves 'perfect' in God's sight by thinking they can live up to God's holy standards and by exerting effort trying to change themselves – 'If only I can break this habit or if only I can resist this temptation' – or by trying to memorise Scripture, attending Bible seminars, paying their tithes, or joining a reclusive order. Some have a long checklist of things they need to follow or obey in order to be acceptable before a holy God. This legalistic thinking is like encountering potholes in the road. It leads the traveller only to discouragement, guilt and disillusionment when they try to complete the tasks and fail.

An engineer friend tells me that these potholes are called 'black holes' (depressions in the road) and that black holes are formed due to fatigue in the road surface. We too can get fatigued easily on this journey if all we are doing is living by a set of rules instead of having a heart towards God with the desire to fulfil his will.

So holiness is not simply a matter of the right language, or habits, or recreation, or clothes, or friends but, because holiness is in the heart, it affects all of these things and many more.

Are you ready to take the journey? Let's take it together.

The first step on the journey is to come to know Christ

No one can take this journey except they know Jesus Christ as their personal Saviour. 'For the grace of God that brings salvation has appeared to all men' (Titus 2:11 *NIV 1984*).

The ultimate purpose or goal of your salvation is to become like Jesus. 'For those God foreknew he also predestined to be conformed to the image of his Son, that he might be the firstborn among many brothers and sisters' (Romans 8:29).

For those of you who are thinking 'Is there something that I need to do?', yes, there is. God has already done his part, he has set you apart; now your part is to set yourselves apart for his use. Say, 'I want to be used by God.'

As we sometimes sing, in the words of chorus No 71 in *The Song Book of The Salvation Army (SASB)*, 'I want to live right, that God may use me at any time and anywhere.'

Just in case you're thinking that you might be in this all by yourself, God has organised your own personal tour guide. He gives you the Holy Spirit. 'It is God's will that you should be sanctified' (1 Thessalonians 4:3). 'But you will receive power when the Holy Spirit comes on you; and you will be my witnesses in Jerusalem, and in all Judea and Samaria, and to the ends of the Earth' (Acts 1:8).

If you are going to be a Christian you don't have a choice as to whether or not you want to be holy. Once you have accepted that, your journey is going to be much easier.

Is that a decision you need to make today, to set yourself apart to God, to ask the Holy Spirit to equip you for the journey? You'll need Jesus as your companion and guide.

There's an old gospel song that says, 'I must have the Saviour with me, for I dare not walk alone' (*SASB* No 731). This is not a solo trip.

The second step in the journey is to be 'others'-oriented

Every time you encounter another person you have the opportunity to practise holiness. The goal of holy living is to live in such a way that others see that you are different.

We once lived in a region where there were many groups belonging to a particular sect. The women had to wear dowdy-looking clothes, their hair long and covered in scarves to signify their submission to God and their husbands. They always looked extremely sad and downtrodden and never exhibited any joy in their lives. They were not allowed to speak to 'others', let alone do anything for 'others'. They set themselves apart by living in communal camps. They had the appearance of being holy but I was reminded of the verse from 2 Timothy 3:5, 'having a form of godliness but denying its power'.

When we talk about 'others', Jesus defined holiness as being a servant. A servant's job is to serve the master but the servant also does the master's bidding and serves others. Jesus said, 'Anyone who wants to be first must be the very last, and the servant of all' (Mark 9:35).

Jesus exemplified this at the last supper when he washed the disciples' feet. This was the ultimate act of humility. It was also a way of showing us that we will occasionally sin as we take this journey, spiritually we will get our feet dirty and will need him to make us completely clean again. That's why Jesus told Peter that if he did not wash his feet he would have no part with him.

A number of years ago I was in a group of tourists travelling down the coastal Broad Beach area in California. We seated ourselves at some tables along the roadway and snapped our fingers for service. Water and bread were placed on the table for us, cloths for washing our hands were provided, and before long the meal we had ordered arrived and was beautifully served. When it was time to pay, the 'servants' standing alongside our table told us there was no charge as they had been happy to serve us. We were somewhat bewildered by this and, on asking the owner why, we soon discovered that we had mistaken his home for a roadside café. His family had served us without any question!

I learned a lesson that day. We can say we practise being servants, when in reality it's not until we live like that man and his family that we become servants, ready to serve the master without question in a spirit of holiness. The evidence of holiness is displayed in how we perceive people and how we treat others.

How do people who have set themselves apart act in order to do as God does?

God demonstrated this for us in two practical ways; by loving others and by forgiving others.

We need to love others as God has loved us. How did God love us? 'For God so loved the world that he gave his one and only Son, that whoever believes in him shall not perish but have eternal life' (John 3:16).

You can't love others until you learn to love God with all your heart, soul, mind and strength, otherwise your words and actions will be hollow. In 1 Corinthians 13:1 we read, 'If I speak in the tongues of men or of angels, but do not have love, I am only a resounding gong or a clanging cymbal.'

Once we learn to love God and know what breaks his heart, we will want to forgive others. Let me ask you a question. How much has God forgiven you? The answer should be *everything*! If God has forgiven us everything then how much are we to forgive others? How many times are we to forgive? Peter came to Jesus and asked the same question in Matthew 18:21-22, '"Lord, how many times shall I forgive my brother or sister who sins against me? Up to seven times?" Jesus answered, "I tell you, not seven times, but seventy-seven times."'

As we know, on a journey there may be roadblocks, hidden dangers and predators lurking just around the corner. The main danger is predictable and we have been alerted early to the warning signs and his tactics and the action we need to take. 'Be self-controlled and alert. Your enemy the devil prowls around like a roaring lion looking for someone to devour' (1 Peter 5:8 *NIV 1984*).

Let me give you some roadblocks to watch out for on your journey. Unlike roads that have a rock fall or subsidence (cave-in), or a bridge washout, we can't put up a detour sign. The obstructions must be totally removed. We cannot manoeuvre around such things.

Obstructions such as unforgiveness: 'And when you stand praying, if you hold anything against anyone, forgive them, so that your Father in Heaven may forgive you your sins' (Mark 11:25). If you find that you cannot forgive others, then it's a sure indication that you have not received the forgiveness of God for yourself.

Obstructions such as ego or pride: 'Be kindly affectionate one to another with brotherly love; in honour preferring one another' (Romans 12:10 *AKJV*). This is an act of humility. Remember when I mentioned about Jesus washing the disciples' feet? He demonstrated the need to humble ourselves. 'Humble yourselves, therefore, under God's mighty hand, that he may lift you up in due time' (1 Peter 5:6).

Obstructions such as unconfessed sin: 'I have hidden your word in my heart that I might not sin against you' (Psalm 119:11). God cannot be in the presence of sin and we need to cleanse ourselves of everything that would separate us from him. Remember the original text: '...say "no" to ungodliness and worldly passions, and to live self-controlled, upright and godly lives in this present age' (Titus 2:12-13).

If you encounter any of these roadblocks, your relationship with God will be interrupted and you will need to act fast to repair the connection in order to resume your journey.

God has saved us and set us apart for his use. We need to decide whether we want to be used by God and then take the necessary steps so we can be used by him.

A final prayer
Father, I pray that those reading this message will release their hearts to you and allow themselves to be your vessels consecrated and set apart to you. I pray that we will reflect your holiness while we wait for the blessed hope – at your glorious appearing! In Jesus name, amen.

Major Stacy Birks
USA Western Territory

A City of Refuge

Romans 8:1-17, Numbers chapter 35, Joshua chapter 20,
Deuteronomy chapter 19, Exodus 21:12-13

DO you ever need to get away from it all? Do you find yourself wanting a place to escape to? Would you like to spend time in a hideaway where you can catch your breath, compose yourself and think clearly? Is there a place of safety and compassion for you to retreat to? A place of protection where you can be free – free from fear and retribution? That's a city of refuge!

I found such a sanctuary in Edmonds, Washington, USA. It was called Rosary Heights. A quiet place. A place of beauty. Fifteen acres of peaceful gardens, an historic mansion with sweeping views of Puget Sound where I could sit on a bench with my sack lunch and watch ferryboats go by. It was a place for retreat, a place to meditate, and to pray. There was no judging, just acceptance. I loved every moment I spent there. I was saddened when I found out it was going to be closed and sold. My city of refuge was going to lock me out forever.

I was saddened because it meant a lot to me and many others who went there seeking refuge. We went there to sit and be quiet, to meditate in the garden, or walk the Stations of the Cross. One woman came to Rosary Heights just to dance in the main room where all the glass windows overlooked the Sound. Others came once a month for Taizé prayers.

In my brooding over this loss, I referred to the Bible (something I did often at Rosary Heights). I read the Psalms because I can always find one

7

to match my mood. Psalm 46:1 says, 'God is our refuge and strength, an ever-present help in trouble.'

God is my refuge and strength! God – through Jesus – provides refuge for me. He provides safety and compassion. He provides protection. He helps me to be free from fear and retribution. Rosary Heights was a special place of refuge when I needed a place to get away and meet with God, but it wasn't the place that did anything, it was the Holy Spirit of Jesus in me that provided sanctuary.

As human beings we think we need people to talk to, things to touch, places to go, but as followers of Jesus we have faith in God, '...confidence in what we hope for and assurance about what we do not see' (Hebrews 11:1). All we really need is the Lord. Proverbs 18:10 says it best, 'The name of the Lord is a fortified tower; the righteous run to it and are safe.'

As we look at the cities of refuge in the Old Testament, my hope is we will discover that 'in Christ' every believer can find a place of safety and security. My prayer is that we discover, too, that our church is to be a refuge for the people in our community.

Cities of refuge were established by Moses for the people of Israel – a direct request from God. Israel was a new nation and it didn't take too long to discover it needed laws and a judicial system. These cities of refuge were instituted to provide asylum for people who were entitled to protection. Look at a few passages that explain: Numbers 35:9-15; Joshua 20:1-6; Deuteronomy 19; Exodus 21:12-13. They were important to God so we need to look at them closely.

These six cities – three on the east of the Jordan River and three on the west – were accessible to all. Both Jews and Gentiles were welcome. Cities of refuge were within walking distance of any city. They were built on a hill to be easily seen. They gave shelter from an avenger, protecting someone who accidentally committed homicide. The accused had to remain in the city if he wanted protection, until the reigning high priest died. The names of the cities meant 'holy', 'shoulder', 'fellowship', 'fortified place', 'height', 'joy' – all names that would have special meaning to those who needed a place of refuge.

Like the cities of refuge, Jesus is our refuge. As we read in Romans 8:1

NLT, 'There is no condemnation for those who belong to Christ Jesus.' He is our refuge and strength. He is a strong tower. It is not enough to just know of Jesus, or read the Bible, or memorise doctrine. We are to go to him and remain there, or abide with him.

When my youngest daughter was in fifth and sixth year of school we used to invite the neighbourhood children to our home after school on Fridays for Bible club. We taught a Bible lesson, provided snacks, crafts, and led songs. It was a fun way to end the week. Some days we would have a dozen young people. One Friday, one of the boys, Billy, asked Jesus to come into his life. It was after we shared a lot of warm homemade bread and butter together. Then, we talked about Jesus being our Bread of Life. Billy understood. It was a beautiful moment when we prayed the following prayer together:

> *Dear Jesus, I believe that you are the Bread of Life. I'm sorry for the wrong things I've done. I know that I won't have everything I need in my life unless you are a part of me. I need you most of all. Please be my best friend. Please help me know what's right. Please help me want what's right. Thank you, Jesus. Amen!*

I explained to the children that if one of them prayed that prayer, God was giving him or her a new life. An 11-year-old went to the city of refuge! He knew he was a sinner and he wanted to accept God's grace of forgiveness and salvation.

The cities of refuge were for everyone and anyone who needed them. They were accessible, on a hill or a mountain. Jesus is for everyone. We are to lift up Jesus so that all may come to him.

Matthew 5:14-16 says, 'You are the light of the world. A town built on a hill cannot be hidden. Neither do people light a lamp and put it under a bowl. Instead they put it on its stand, and it gives light to everyone in the house. In the same way, let your light shine before others, that they may see your good deeds and glorify your Father in Heaven.'

Christ is a city of refuge to sinners, which means all of us. He is available to those who desire to flee the death and judgement we deserve

9

because of our sin. Every believer can have security and safety in Christ. He does not condemn but offers refuge and sanctuary, freedom from fear and retribution, protection and safety.

As we take refuge in Christ, we will want to offer the same to others. Our churches can be cities of refuge. All who have Jesus in our lives bring him with us wherever we go. We are to lift him up and share him with those who also need a 'city of refuge' from the world. We are to be 'generous with your lives' (Matthew 5:14-16 *TM*). God is our refuge and strength. He is our ever-present help in trouble. I hope and pray Jesus is your city of refuge. If not, go to him and receive him today.

You may already know about Jesus and have experienced him as your refuge. If so, I hope you continue to share his peace and love with others.

There is a story told about cities of refuge. Every year on a designated day, it was the law that all citizens would go out of the cities and clean up the roads leading to the cities of refuge. The people would make sure the signs were repaired and easily seen and the roads were clearly marked.

You and I, as citizens of God's Kingdom, are compelled to do the same. We should clear any obstacle on the path to Jesus found in our lives. We don't want to be the reason someone never hears about the Lord. Let us lift him up, the Light of the World, and offer the Jesus, the city of refuge, to someone today.

Captain Robyn Black
Australia Eastern Territory

Choosing to Respond

Acts 16:16-26

LIFE can often take unexpected twists and turns. Sometimes we are sure that God is leading us in a particular direction, we're sure we've heard from him, and we expect to be a part of great things for the Kingdom of God. But life is rarely so straightforward, and we often have to cope with unexpected delays and uncertainties along the way.

Paul and Silas found themselves in a Philippian jail on a trumped up charge. Earlier, Paul had ordered a demonic spirit out of a slave girl, in the name of Jesus Christ, and her owners were not at all happy. The young girl was wonderfully released from her oppression. Unfortunately, she had ceased to be a source of income for her owners, and in their fury they accused Paul and Silas of being anti-Roman. The Romans were the occupying force in the area, which meant the military force was Roman, the government was Roman, the engineers designing the roads were Roman and the magistrate was Roman. Philippi was a Roman colony and Rome was all-powerful.

Paul and Silas had disturbed the Philippian crowd, but no doubt they would have expected that, as they were in a Roman colony, preaching freedom in Christ. They were in a city oppressed by an all-powerful hierarchical system, bringing a message that the first shall be last and the last shall be first. They were in a city where Caesar reigned supreme, and they were telling listeners that the Kingdom of God is above all. They were bound to upset people, to make them uncomfortable and uneasy.

The Kingdom of God was counter-cultural, that is, completely

11

different to the accepted culture of the time. And, praise God, the good news of Christ continues to be counter-cultural today.

Paul and Silas were not given a trial but were stripped and beaten unmercifully with rods first. *The Message* paraphrase says that, 'The judges went along with the mob, had Paul and Silas's clothes ripped off and ordered a public beating. After beating them black-and-blue, they threw them into jail, telling the jailkeeper to put them under heavy guard so there would be no chance of escape. He did just that – threw them into the maximum security cell in the jail and clamped leg irons on them' (Acts 16:22-24).

The prisons in Philippi were like dug-out dungeons, little more than rat-infested, cold and dark holes. Paul and Silas were put into the 'inner cell' (Acts 16:24) of the prison, that is, the most difficult cell to escape from and, therefore, the most secure part of the prison. The magistrate clearly didn't want to take any chances with Paul and Silas. Perhaps he was more than a bit fearful of the power seen at work in the life of the slave girl.

Paul and Silas had been severely beaten. Their bodies were aching, their open wounds were untended, and their feet were in stocks. This was unfair treatment – they were bringing news of new life in Christ, a peaceful revolution of the heart, but the people of Philippi responded with fear and insecurity. We often respond with fear and insecurity when we're faced with something new, challenging or different.

Do you wonder if, at the midnight hour, Paul and Silas might have been justified in questioning God's plans? At that moment, sitting in the pitch-black prison, their legs in chains, do you wonder what their thoughts were? It would have been reasonable to be completely focused on their pain and suffering. They would have been justified in wondering why God had directed them to Macedonia and Philippi just to end up broken and beaten in jail. If Paul and Silas had doubted if they had really heard from God, who would have blamed them? They didn't know what was in store for them, or what the future would hold.

I used to work at a 24-hour per day Salvation Army telephone counselling service. For a while I worked the 1am to 9am shift. There are a lot of people awake at that time of night. Most people who phoned the service in the middle of the night were worried about their circumstances in life, completely focused on their own pain and suffering. This is a reasonable response – it can be difficult to sleep when you're going over and over your problems in your mind. There's something about night-time that magnifies problems, making the way forward seem uncertain.

Paul and Silas chose to respond in a positive way to the problems which beset them. There is no doubt that, if they had allowed their feelings to dictate how they responded, they would have been very angry. Paul was a man whose natural inclination was to be judgemental and self-righteous. Paul had been raised and trained as a Pharisee (Galatians 1:14). In Philippians 3:5-6 *NIV 1984*, Paul describes himself as 'a Hebrew of Hebrews'; in regard to the law, 'a Pharisee...as for legalistic righteousness, faultless.'

Paul was raised in a legalistic environment. He knew the Law of Moses, and would have been familiar with the law of Rome. For Paul, everything was black or white, right or wrong, and there were no grey areas. It would have been easy for him to inwardly fume about this humiliating and unjust treatment. I think Paul and Silas would have been justified in being a little self-obsessed at this point.

The writer of the book of Acts tells us, 'About midnight Paul and Silas were praying and singing hymns to God' (Acts 16:25). Instead of getting angry or resentful, Paul and Silas chose to pray and sing hymns to God. Paul knew the Old Testament Scriptures like the back of his hand, and he would have remembered Psalm 40 well: 'I waited patiently for the Lord; he turned to me and heard my cry. He lifted me out of the slimy pit, out of the mud and mire; he set my feet on a rock and gave me a firm place to stand' (Psalm 40:1-2).

This psalm talks about being in a slimy pit. When I read this psalm, I've always imagined being stuck at the bottom of a well, where you just can't get a grip on to the walls. I picture a very deep well, where the walls are slimy and there's absolutely no way of climbing out by myself and I am completely powerless.

Like the Psalmist, we will all face situations that we are unable to resolve in our own strength. No matter how clever or strong we are, there will be times when we are powerless. Perhaps you are in the midst of illness or financial difficulty, or grieving the loss of a loved one, and feeling vulnerable and alone. God is there to help you. Psalm 40 affirms that God is the one who can lift us out of that slimy pit. God is our deliverer, our rock and the strength of our life. I can imagine Paul reciting this psalm, believing that God could and would deliver them. They understood that they were completely powerless in their own strength, and that God was their only hope. They made a choice to 'wait patiently for the Lord' (v 1) and call upon his name in prayer.

The Scripture also tells us that Paul and Silas were 'singing hymns to God'. In some ways I find it difficult to comprehend Paul and Silas' singing while they were in this state. But, you know, Paul would have known the rest of Psalm 40, and during his life would have often recited the comforting words of verse three; 'He put a new song in my mouth, a hymn of praise to our God. Many will see and fear the Lord and put their trust in him.'

Choosing to respond positively in difficult times is not always easy. It's far easier to go with the flow, to allow our feelings to dictate our responses. On reflection of my response to a particular situation recently, I acknowledged once more that every challenge is an opportunity to respond as God would have me do.

I can feel justified in reacting with indignation or resentment or with a lack of empathy to people or situations, with logical arguments for my behaviour. But at the end of the day, the only question I need to answer is: am I responding as Jesus would have?

Every difficulty is an opportunity for us to ask: have I behaved in a Christlike manner? We should be mindful of the fact that it's never too late to say I'm sorry, I haven't responded as God would want me to, or to confess to God, Lord, I'm sorry I haven't responded to this challenge in a way that honours you.

Jesus was never provoked to anger when he was treated badly. He was never indignant when people misunderstood him. He didn't go off and sulk. He only ever became angry when God was disrespected or misrepresented.

I think that sometimes we have to deliberately battle our egos as there is that part within us that craves recognition, and that needs others to know we've made a sacrifice for them and how much they've inconvenienced us. We justify our bad temper by going over our frustrations, and our egos tell us we are 'at liberty' to respond in this way.

But in the midst of this most difficult situation, Paul and Silas chose to respond in a way that honoured God. They chose to focus on God in prayer and worship. 'About midnight Paul and Silas were praying and singing hymns to God, and the other prisoners were listening to them' (Acts 16:25).

Do you ever wonder who is listening in on your conversations? For Paul and Silas, it was the people who were nearest to them. Maybe it annoyed a few of the prisoners who had just managed to nod off. Perhaps some prisoners had heard through the grapevine that Paul and Silas were preaching about a new way of life, a way of grace and love and peace. But talk is cheap, and anyone can say the right things when the prevailing situation is favourable. As the prisoners listened to Paul and Silas sing, they were left in no doubt that Jesus truly made a difference in their lives.

Who is listening to you? It's often the people we live with, the people we work with, the people we are related to, the people we go to university with and the people we live next door to. Who is listening to the way you respond to challenges and difficulties? We may profess Jesus, but do those around us see evidence of the love, the joy, the peace and the patience in our lives when times are tough? Do our friends and family see the transforming power of the Holy Spirit in our lives?

For Paul and Silas 'talking the talk' was one thing, but when they were in dire circumstances, those around them saw – or rather heard – them 'walking the walk'.

We don't always pass the 'walk the walk' test, and those around us are quick to notice if what we say and what we do don't match up. People want to see authenticity, and they want to know that Jesus really does make a difference to how we live.

15

Like Paul and Silas, each one of us will face difficult situations in life. We can find ourselves in a 'jail' of financial debt, depression, loneliness or addiction and shame. Perhaps your 'jail' is an abusive past, or the consequences of making bad decisions, or maybe you are being persecuted for your faith. You may be very aware of your own powerlessness and wondering how you will survive this situation.

The good news is that here is hope. This hope is found in Jesus, who gave his life '...to proclaim good news to the poor...to proclaim freedom for the prisoners and recovery of sight for the blind, to set the oppressed free' (Luke 4:18).

Freedom is found in the powerful name of Jesus, and release from oppression by his precious blood. Whatever situation you are facing, he is sufficient. Whatever circumstance you are facing, he is able. Whatever sorrow you are suffering, he will bear it. He is faithful. He is merciful. He is powerful. He is trustworthy!

If Paul and Silas could speak to us, they would urge us to 'turn our eyes upon Jesus', to choose to worship him in whatever situation we find ourselves. For he will lift us 'out of the slimy pit, out of the mud and mire', and he will 'set my feet upon a rock'. All praise to his glorious name!

Major Patricia Brown
*United Kingdom Territory with
the Republic of Ireland*

Standing in the Gap

Ezekiel 22:30, Psalm 106:19-23, Acts 3:1-10

Introduction

ONE of the things I love as we come into a new fellowship and get to know a new family of people is the opportunity to pray together – in conversations, in people's homes, in times of worship, and in quiet moments in the midst of a busy week.

On Thursday mornings the invitation is given to staff and anyone in the building to come and share a few moments of quietness as we read verses from Scripture and pray. It is a blessing to be able to pray together. What a privilege it is to be able to take those moments together and use them in such a positive way. We simply ask for names or situations to be raised up in prayer. I find it a very moving experience.

Very often, for me, it can be a time when tears fall. To be able to pray for each other and with each other is something I hope I never take for granted. It is a blessing and a privilege to be able to lift up someone's name before God and ask God to be with them.

Ezekiel

When the Old Testament prophet Ezekiel began his message, Israel was under attack from Babylon, one of the greatest powers of the day. When the Babylonians conquered a nation, it was their strategy to uproot the local people and resettle them in a different land as captives and slaves. So as a young man of about 30 years of age, Ezekiel had been forcibly deported to Babylon where he continued to speak a message of judgement and destruction.

In the first part of the book we see how he poured out warning after warning. We read of incredible visions and strange symbolism and the amazing things Ezekiel did to try to get people to listen to the word of the Lord.

Ezekiel was a man of God who proclaimed a message that his people really didn't want to hear. They thought things were bad; he told them it would get worse! They thought times were tough; he told them the worst was still to come!

And yet we discover that when the unthinkable had happened and the impossible had come to pass – when the great Temple at Jerusalem had finally been destroyed and the people of God had been divided and scattered – Ezekiel's message of judgement changed (Ezekiel chapters 33-39).

Now it became a message of comfort and hope and promise. One day God would bring his people back to their own land and the terrible things that had happened to divide them would be behind them. One day they would again be united.

Ezekiel's prophecy is not easy to read and not easy to understand, and for the people of his day his message was certainly not welcome. But in the middle of this really hard message there is an interesting text: 'I looked for someone among them who would build up the wall and stand before me in the gap on behalf of the land so I would not have to destroy it, but I found no one' (Ezekiel 22:30).

It was this search for a man to 'stand…in the gap' that caught my interest. What does it mean? God looked for someone to stand in the gap and, through Ezekiel, he declared, 'I found no one'. In the middle of such dreadful times, no one was there to stand in the gap on behalf of the people of God.

Moses
Centuries before Ezekiel, another man of God, Moses, stood in the breach; he stood in the gap for the people of God.

18

The Psalmist remembered the old story and summarised it for us in Psalm 106:19-23. Isn't that amazing? God said he would destroy his rebellious people 'had not Moses, his chosen one, stood in the breach' (v 23). Moses stood in the gap between God and the people, and he prayed on their behalf.

Moses stood in a place of prayer somewhere between a holy God and a sinful people and asked the Lord for mercy. God answered his prayer and he showed his mercy. Moses knew what it was to stand in the gap.

Are there times when we are required to stand in the gap for someone? Times when we are called to intercede on behalf of others? Times when we must stand in the gap and fulfil a need for someone who might not be able to do that for themselves?

Peter

Let's look at the New Testament story from Acts 3:1-10. It is the familiar story of a lame man lying at the gate to the temple begging for money.

This man had been at the temple gate every day for years. Every day someone would bring him to the gates so that he could ask for money from those who were going in.

In those days there were people who thought that any handicap or deformity or sickness was a punishment for sin, either your own or your parents'. But Peter and John just didn't accept that this man *deserved* to be where he was because of sin. In fact, they didn't condemn or criticise or judge him at all – they simply stood in the gap on his behalf.

And look at how they did it; look how Peter and John interacted with this man. They stopped and commanded the man to look up at them. He had obviously seen them coming; he had asked them for money but he didn't really give them his full attention. So Peter looked straight at him and said, 'Look at us!' (v 4).

Then once he had his full attention, Peter said to the man, 'Silver or gold I do not have, but what I do have I give you. In the name of Jesus Christ of Nazareth, walk' (v 6).

What did Peter have? He had Jesus Christ. He told the man in the name of Jesus to get up and walk.

Here is the good part. Peter didn't wait for the man to think about what he had said or call a friend. The man didn't wait for the crowd to have their say. He didn't wait for the crowd to discuss the man's condition. He immediately reached down and picked the man up. 'Taking him by the right hand, he helped him up, and instantly the man's feet and ankles became strong' (v 7).

We can see how Peter stood in the gap for this lame man – one hand to the man, the other reaching towards God. He literally stood in the gap and helped the man on to his feet.

When Peter spoke to this man, he had no doubt that he would be healed. When Peter spoke to this man, he spoke as an equal – without criticism or judgement. When Peter spoke to this man, he simply wanted to do what he knew God would have him do.

If you and I are to be effective in standing in the gap for anyone, we need to come with that same attitude. We need to believe that other people deserve God's grace as much as we do. We need to believe that, even if what has happened to them appears self-inflicted or can be justified in some way, they don't need to be blamed; they don't need to be criticised. They need our compassion.

We come not to judge or condemn. We come only to stand in the gap for them. We simply come believing God wants the best for them.

You and me

Sometimes though, we admit, it seems very hard to stand in the gap for someone else. There may be lots of reasons for this.

Sometimes we find it hard to stand in the gap for someone else because we are struggling with our own needs and our own disappointments and our own hurts, and we feel we have enough to cope with.

When we feel under attack from every side, or we don't feel we have the inner resources to pray for someone else, we need to remember that very often that's the time when someone else is standing in the gap for us.

Many of us have known the power of having someone else stand in the gap for us. We have known the rich benefits of that simple phrase 'I'm praying for you' and we know how much it means to be told that someone else holds us in their heart, and that someone is standing in the gap for us. It gives us such strength and encouragement.

Even in our own difficult times we are called to do the same for others. It does us good to focus on the needs of someone else, confident that someone is standing in the gap for us. We are here for each other. We do not live in isolation.

Conclusion

I believe God is calling us today to stand in the gap – for our families, our friends, our work colleagues and our leaders. He calls us to stand in the gap for all those in positions of influence or government or authority. He calls us to stand in the gap as a bridge between them and God.

In the days of Ezekiel, God was searching for someone to stand in the gap for his people. He found no one. God needs to be able to find in us someone prepared to stand in the gap, someone spiritually equipped and willing to step up and intercede for the needs of others.

God is looking for those who are willing to stand for those who cannot stand for themselves. The question is, are you and I willing to commit to stand in the gap?

Captain Leanne Browski
Southern Africa Territory

Mothers with a Message for Today

Matthew 1:1-17

Introduction

THE children in a prominent family decided to give their father a book of the family's history as a birthday present. They commissioned a professional biographer to do the work, carefully warning him of the family's 'black sheep'. Uncle George had been executed, in the electric chair, for murder. The biographer assured the children, 'I can handle that situation so that there will be no embarrassment. I'll merely say that Uncle George occupied a chair of applied electronics at an important government institution. He was attached to his position by the strongest of ties and that his death came as a real shock.'

You know the old saying, 'You can pick and choose your friends but you can't pick your family.' Since it is Mother's Day I felt led to look at Jesus' family tree, in particular the women who are mentioned in Jesus' genealogy, to see what we can learn from them.

You would think, when it comes to Jesus' heritage, the choice of people in his family tree would show pure breeding lines – only the best to prepare the way for the Son of God. It is interesting to note that this is not the case and that conniving, sinful, foreign, adulterous and very ordinary people make up his bloodline.

Let us look a little closer.

Tamar

The first woman mentioned is Tamar, the mother of Perez and Zerah. She is probably best known for her determination and for orchestrating circumstances – conniving might be a more descriptive word – to get what she wanted in order to be in right standing in terms of family and society. Genesis 38 tells Tamar's story. She was a heathen girl, married to Er the firstborn son of Judah. Unfortunately Er died without producing an heir. Culture and custom dictated that Tamar should marry one of Judah's other sons and conceive a child, so that Er's name would continue. Judah and his sons were not terribly excited at the prospect, and as a result Tamar remained childless.

Tamar, desperate and determined, dressed as a harlot and seduced Judah, and as a result of their union she conceived her father-in-law's child. This almost sounds like a storyline for a soap opera. As we read the account in Genesis we realise that Tamar was prepared to go to extreme lengths to get what she wanted in order to be in right standing in her community.

Tamar's actions very nearly cost her her life. While we might frown somewhat at Tamar's behaviour, there are occasions when we are no different. We may sometimes go to extreme lengths to secure our future, making compromises, bending the truth or riding roughshod over somebody to get what we want. As Christians we do not need to behave in this manner. We can trust God with our future. One of my favourite verses in Scripture is Psalm 138:8 *NIV 1984*, 'The Lord will fulfil his purpose for me; your love, O Lord, endures forever'. The Lord will fulfil his purpose for me so I don't need to worry about my future because God's got that covered. It is not necessary to manipulate people or situations because he is in control. Let us rest in the knowledge that God is more than able to fulfil his purpose for our lives because of his love that endures forever.

Rahab

Rahab is mentioned next in Jesus' genealogy. Rahab lived on the outskirts of the city right on the city wall, but she was also on the outskirts of society. As a prostitute she was an outcast – used, abused and rejected by many. Regardless of who she was and what she had done, she found salvation and favour with God.

The story in Joshua chapter two tells how she hid two spies, sent by Joshua, to scope out the land of Jericho. The inhabitants of Jericho knew about the Israelites and lived in fear of them, Rahab included! We read about this in Joshua 2:11 *NIV 1984*, 'When we heard of it, our hearts melted and everyone's courage failed because of you, for the Lord your God is God in Heaven above and on the Earth below.'

It is interesting to note that, although the people of Jericho were in fear of their lives, Rahab was the only one who turned to God for her salvation. She took a risk and was rewarded. The spies assured her that she and her household would be spared when the Israelites attacked Jericho. She simply needed to tie a scarlet cord in her window. Rahab did as she was told and saved herself and those in her home.

We can learn from Rahab, who did not let her fear affect her faith in God's ability to deliver her. I love the fact that Rahab, incidentally one of only two women to be mentioned in the 'hall of faith' in Hebrews chapter 11, is remembered for her great faith and not her occupation.

The story of Rahab is relevant for us today and challenges us to not let what we are, or what we have done, stand in the way of receiving God's deliverance.

One night in a church service a young woman felt the tug of the Holy Spirit on her heart. She responded to God's call and accepted Jesus as her Lord and Saviour. The young woman had a chequered past, involving alcohol, drugs and prostitution. But the change in her was evident. As time went by she became a faithful member of the church. She eventually became involved in ministry teaching in the Sunday school at the church.

It was not very long before this faithful young woman caught the eye and the heart of the pastor's son. The relationship went from strength to strength and soon they began to make plans for their wedding. This is when the problems began. You see, half the congregation did not think that a woman with a past such as hers was suitable to marry the pastor's son. The other half did, and so the congregation began to argue about the matter. Finally they decided to have a meeting in an attempt to resolve the problem.

As the people made their arguments the tensions increased and the meeting eventually got completely out of control. The young woman became very upset about all the things being raised about her past and began to cry. The pastor's son stood to speak. He could not bear the pain this was causing his future wife. He said: 'My fiancé's past is not what is on trial here. What you are questioning is the ability of the blood of Jesus to wash away sin. Today you have put the blood of Jesus on trial. So, does it wash away sin or not?' A hush descended on the church, and then people began to weep as they realised what they had done.

Don't let your past stand in the way of receiving salvation. The blood of Jesus can wash away your sin.

Ruth

The third woman found in Jesus' family tree is Ruth, well known for the wonderful way in which she stood by her widowed mother-in-law. As we look at Ruth, we see a woman who turned her back on her old life. She was a widowed, pagan, homeless and penniless woman living in a foreign land. Yet she embraced a new life and God, and she was changed forever. We read in Ruth 1:16, 'Where you go I will go, and where you stay I will stay. Your people will be my people and your God my God.'

We can learn a great deal from this remarkable woman. Not simply because she chose to live with her mother-in-law when she could have gone back to her own people, but because she chose to leave her past behind her. We note that if we, like Ruth, turn our backs on our past lives and choose to make the only true and living God our Saviour, he works things out for us. God has a plan and purpose for our lives and as we trust him and follow him his plans will come to fruition.

Ruth's life was changed and she became a God-fearing, blessed woman, married to a wealthy honourable farmer and a member of the Son of God's gene pool.

The story of Ruth gives us great hope, serving as a reminder that we too can make a fresh start and break away from the old life and the same way of doing things. Like Ruth, you can know the blessing and favour of the Lord, as you trust him with your life. You will notice from Ruth's life that the positive changes to her life did not come overnight. God's plan began to unfold as she trusted him and did the right thing. Evidence of his divine hand at work began to show and she experienced God's ability to transform her life for the better.

Bathsheba

Bathsheba is next in line. It is interesting to note that, although she is mentioned, it is not by name – she is referred to as the mother of Solomon, who had been Uriah's wife. The story of Bathsheba is found in 2 Samuel chapter 11. She was a beautiful woman who caught King David's eye as she was taking a bath and, although she was married, she had an affair with David and conceived his child. This adulterous act ultimately led to the murder of her husband Uriah.

We learn from Bathsheba that the consequences of sin are enormous. Her sin resulted in the murder of her innocent husband and the death of her child. Bathsheba heralds a warning to resist temptation because it hurts us and harms others. It is clear from her life that we don't escape our transgression and the consequences are painful, causing brokenness and distress. Let us learn from Bathsheba not to indulge in the pleasures that sin offers, because the penalty is great.

Bathsheba also shares another message, one of hope, because although the consequences of sin are immense God's forgiveness is greater. God is able cleanse us from our sin and allows good to come out of these situations. This story is also about God's forgiveness. Once there was true repentance by David and Bathsheba, God forgave their sin and blessed their lives with a son, Solomon.

Mary

Our last, but probably most well-known, woman in Jesus' family tree is his mother, Mary. We know Mary's story fairly well: a young woman engaged to be married has an encounter with an angel who informs her of God's amazing plan of salvation and the role she was going to play in it. Young, ordinary Mary, with an extraordinary desire to serve God, submits to the will of God for her life.

I love this story, not only because it is the Christmas story, with the wonderful truth of a loving God who wants to be reconciled with the people he loves, but also because it reminds me that God's best servants are often ordinary people like ourselves.

We live in a world that has a natural selection process of always choosing the biggest, brightest and best, forgetting that God often uses the simple things of the world to confound the wise. Mary had what it took – we read in Luke 1:38 *NIV 1984*: "'I am the Lord's servant," Mary answered, "may it be to me as you have said"'.

Maybe you want to make yourself available to God; perhaps your desire is to make a difference in your family life, where you live and in the workplace. Why not repeat Mary's words that echo down the walls of time: 'I am the Lord's servant…may it be to me as you have said.' We need to ask ourselves whether we are prepared to do what Mary did, whatever it is that the Lord requires.

Conclusion

With which of these five women do you identify? Is it Tamar? Are you so afraid of what the future holds that you find yourself frantically scurrying around, trying to make your own plans, putting things in place in an effort to control or secure what tomorrow will hold. You may not go to the same lengths she was prepared to, but you worry and you stress and you find yourself going to great lengths to sort out tomorrow, before it has even happened. If this describes how you feel, take comfort from Psalm 138:8 *NIV 1984*: 'The Lord will fulfil his purpose for me; your love, O Lord, endures forever…'. As a child of God you don't need to be anxious about the future. God, your loving heavenly Father, has a plan for your life and as you walk in obedience with him he will fulfil those plans for you.

Perhaps you can identify with of Rahab – you have a chequered past and your future is not bright. Why not take your example from Rahab and allow your faith and trust in God to lift you out of your circumstances?

Don't allow yourself to be trapped in a downward spiral when God is able to deliver you.

The story of Ruth's new life and hope may have inspired you to want to start afresh, even though you are not sure where it may lead you. God, who led Ruth through some difficult times, has not changed and when you commit your life to him he will not fail you. Now is the time to embrace the life that God offers you through Christ Jesus.

The story of Bathsheba's life may have struck a chord with you, as a warning to resist the allure of sin. Your situation may warrant the need to repent so that you can experience God's forgiveness. Remember there is no sin committed that Jesus' blood cannot cover. Call on him.

Finally, perhaps you have an affinity with Mary. You see yourself as one of the run-of-the-mill and yet you earnestly yearn to do God's will. Be courageous and take your lead from Mary by dedicating your life to God. Pray these simple yet life-changing words: 'I am the Lord's servant...may it be to me as you have said'.

We have been able to learn a little from each of these women. Each has undergone a life-changing experience as a result of their relationship with God. Let us heed the advice from these seasoned mothers and respond readily to God.

Lieut-Colonel Susan Bukiewicz
USA Central Territory

Make Me a Captive, Lord!

Jeremiah chapter 29

'OH they hung their harps on the weeping willow tree and dared not sing 'til they were free', was a little ditty my father used to sing when we were little girls. The melody was lilting and fun. My sisters and I were pretty sure he had made it up but even as a child I knew the words did not match the happy tune. There was something wrong with people who had harps but wouldn't sing.

It wasn't until I was grown and more familiar with the history of God's chosen people that I put the little song from my childhood together with what I had read in Jeremiah 29. Then, during a difficult season in my service as an officer, God used this Scripture to speak to my soul.

At the time of Jeremiah, Nebuchadnezzar had developed a policy of resettlement for troublesome ethnic groups in his empire. If a people rebelled, he simply took them from their homeland. He intended to neutralise their patriotism and, in time, to blot out their identity.

In an age when the gods of a people were thought to own their particular territory, deportation undermined their religious faith. Typically, exiles began to worship the gods and goddesses of the new land where they were settled. In the ancient world it was politically correct to be on good terms with the deities who owned the area in which one lived.

The Babylonian captivity was a turning point for the people of Judah. God had finally had it. He is too pure to look on while evil reigns. He cannot tolerate wrong and finally acted to punish and judge his sinning people.

As we read the stories of men and women associated with this period of history, we make several significant discoveries.

First, the captivity was not a single event but rather took place over a 19-year period through a series of deportations of Jews to Babylon. Groups were taken in 605, 597 and 586 BC. The first deportation took upper-class persons, the second seemingly focused on artisans and leaders, and the third – some 70,000 persons – included all but the 'poor' who later fled to Egypt.

We know Daniel, Shadrach, Meshach and Abednego were taken captive and forced to serve King Nebuchadnezzar. But Daniel had prestigious administrative duties for 60 years! The famous account of Daniel in the lions' den happened when the prophet was an old man, more than 80 years of age, around 536 BC.

Second, the 'return' was not a single event or mass movement. Two large groups of people moved from Babylon to the Holy Land, the first in 538 BC and the second some 80 years later in 458 BC. During this period and beyond it there were more Jews outside the Holy Land than in it!

Third, the focus of history had shifted from the land of Palestine itself to the Gentile world powers.

So there they were, God's chosen people, torn from the Promised Land and suddenly aware of the depth of their sins against God. They lived in material comfort but spiritual pain.

Jeremiah 29:1-4; 'This is the text of the letter that the prophet Jeremiah sent from Jerusalem to the surviving elders among the exiles and to the priests, the prophets and all the other people Nebuchadnezzar had carried into exile from Jerusalem to Babylon. (This was after King Jehoiachin and the queen mother, the court officials and the leaders of Judah and Jerusalem, the skilled workers and the craftsmen had gone into exile from Jerusalem.) He entrusted the letter to Elasah son of Shaphan and to Gemariah son of Hilkiah, whom Zedekiah king of Judah sent to King Nebuchadnezzar in Babylon. It said: "This is what the Lord Almighty, the God of Israel, says to all those I carried into exile from Jerusalem to Babylon."'

The Lord Almighty is a military term chosen to show God as the general, commanding the hosts of Heaven against his enemy. Scripture says the Lord Almighty carried the Israelites into exile! God needed his people to understand that this was not a mistake, not a weakness in the plan or character of God. The general of the hosts of Heaven deliberately carried his people into a pagan, hostile place.

The irony is that ruthless King Nebuchadnezzar historically conquered and deported people. It was not enough for him to physically harm, he also wanted to inflict psychological damage by taking people from their homes by military force. This is the background from which Almighty God told his people that the general of the hosts of Heaven was actually carrying the children of Israel into exile, not a human king! There is no conquering of the children of God by an enemy then – or now.

Now that the question of who was responsible for the Israelites being carried into exile is settled, and the knowledge that it is not a mistake is realised, what did God say to his devastated people? 'Build houses and settle down; plant gardens and eat what they produce' (v 5).

The captives were taken to the capital city of Babylon itself. This was nothing like Egypt for them! They were settled in several districts and the land they lived on was fertile and under irrigation. They worked on the king's building projects. Some at least entered business as merchants. The Babylonians kept careful records, and recovered records show Jewish names on copies of various business transactions. At least one trading house was owned and operated by Jews.

We know from both Jeremiah's and Ezekiel's writings that Jews were allowed much self-government. The community had its own elders, and priests and prophets continued to play an influential role.

Yet despite the material benefits of life in Babylon, those who loved God still experienced those decades as punishment. But remember, God carried them there! God's people were far away from the land of promise, uprooted from their past, and far from the place where the promised Messiah was to appear. They were in a pagan culture; their beautiful place of worship had been destroyed and pilfered. Yet God was telling them to 'settle in'. God was giving them a life where they were.

As a new officer I had many days of discouragement, thinking I did not have the gifts and graces necessary for officership. One day, in a moment of despair, I called my officer-mother for advice. I ended my long list of grievances by saying, 'Mom, I just need to get a life'. She replied, 'This is your life'! That advice was just what I needed to get back on track and settle into a difficult appointment that eventually became a place of joy for my husband and me.

'Marry and have sons and daughters; find wives for your sons and give your daughters in marriage, so that they too may have sons and daughters. Increase in number there; do not decrease' (v 6). Establish a faithful community, one of fidelity in the midst of a pagan society! 'Also, seek the peace and prosperity of the city to which I have carried you into exile. Pray to the Lord for it, because if it prospers, you too will prosper' (v 7). Now this was just too much for me. 'I'll live here Lord. I'll be faithful to you, but don't ask me to seek the peace and prosperity of this evil city filled with evil people who care nothing about you or your commands. I'll live here, but don't expect me to like it!'

God expected his children would obey the laws and submit to the civil authority over them. When asked to bow to the image of a false god, there were those for whom this was not even thinkable. We read the account of the fiery furnace in Scripture that shows God's intervention and protection.

Let me state the obvious: in captivity it is difficult not to have a bad attitude, to put conditions on our obedience and to do the right thing begrudgingly. It was no different for the children of Israel.

In Psalm 137:1-6 we see the attitude of the Israelites, 'By the rivers of Babylon we sat and wept when we remembered Zion. There on the poplars we hung our harps, for there our captors asked us for songs, our tormentors demanded songs of joy; they said, "Sing us one of the songs of Zion!" How can we sing the songs of the Lord while in a foreign land? If I forget you, Jerusalem, may my right hand forget its skill. May my tongue cling to the roof of my mouth if I do not remember you, if I do not consider Jerusalem my highest joy.'

That's cooperation for you!

Again, from Jeremiah we read, 'Yes, this is what the Lord Almighty, the

God of Israel, says: "Do not let the prophets and diviners among you deceive you. Do not listen to the dreams you encourage them to have. They are prophesying lies to you in my name. I have not sent them," declares the Lord' (vv 8-9).

What were these prophets saying to God's people that he judged deceptive? They were telling the Israelites that present circumstances do not matter because God will soon take them back to their home. It was a direct contradiction to what God was telling them: 'This is what the Lord says: "When 70 years are completed for Babylon, I will come to you and fulfil my good promise to bring you back to this place. For I know the plans I have for you," declares the Lord, "plans to prosper you and not to harm you, plans to give you hope and a future."' (vv 10-11).

The promise of a hope and future comes only when we are faithful, patient and God-honouring in captivity. Sometimes our appointments feel like exile. We may be appointed somewhere we just know is a mistake. But God doesn't make mistakes, does he?

"'Then you will call on me and come and pray to me, and I will listen to you. You will seek me and find me when you seek me with all your heart. I will be found by you," declares the Lord, "and will bring you back from captivity. I will gather you from all the nations and places where I have banished you," declares the Lord, "and will bring you back to the place from which I carried you into exile"' (vv 12-14).

The deportation ordered by the Babylonian king Nebuchadnezzar had the opposite effect to what he intended. In Babylon, the faith of the Jewish people was strengthened! And new institutions grew up which would keep that faith vigorous and alive through the centuries that lay ahead.

What about us? Some circumstances feel like captivity. They make no sense to us. But what if God was repeating a strategy that worked for his beloved people thousands of years ago? What if the lives of holiness we are striving to live are best seen in contrast to the pagan culture in which we feel out of place and alienated?

The last thing we should do is 'hang up our harps' and refuse to sing the songs of Zion! Our witness is most powerful against the backdrop of displacement and discouragement, despair and desperation.

My spiritual response to this Scripture is found in the words of George Matheson:

Make me a captive, Lord,
And then I shall be free;
Force me to render up my sword,
And I shall conqueror be.
I sink in life's alarms
When by myself I stand;
Imprison me within thine arms
And strong shall be my hand.

My heart is weak and poor
Until it master find;
It has no spring of action sure,
It varies with the wind.
It cannot freely move
Till thou hast wrought its chain;
Enslave it with thy matchless love
And deathless it shall reign.

My will is not my own
Till thou hast made it thine;
If it would reach a monarch's throne
It must its crown resign;
It only stands unbent
Amid the clashing strife,
When on thy bosom it has leant
And found in thee its life.
SASB, No 508

Major Betzann Carroll
USA Eastern Territory

What is 'Fellowsment'?

1 John 1:1-4

JOHN wants to share with his contemporaries, and with those in generations to come, the truth from his own experience. He wants us to know Christ is God. We need to know Christ and have fellowship with him and find refreshment in him. True joy comes from knowing Christ and living in a nurturing community. This energises us to evangelise.

What is 'fellowsment'? Have you ever heard of the word? I have heard the word but I have never actually seen it in print. 'Fellowsment.'

Our son Stephen started developing a terrific vocabulary at the age of two. While he never played baseball or football on a team because of his heart defect, he could win a race with words every time. He could talk himself out of almost every situation. Essays were a snap – and what a charmer! In one corps he was very successful in getting double portions of chicken by telling three different women they made the *best* fried chicken ever. That is of course until they began comparing notes!

When Stephen was three we were getting ready to celebrate the enrolment of new soldiers at the corps. We were planning a special service and a reception to follow in their honour. We worked hard and Stephen was a part of the preparation. He folded the napkins and polished the chairs.

On the Sunday, following the service, he wanted to make the announcement. In his formal little voice he said, 'Attention please! We have fellowsment in the other room. We have napkins and everything so come on everybody!'

He was ready to eat. He was also excited to be with his favourite people and enjoy their company, to listen to their stories and laugh at their jokes. He had 'fellowsment'.

Fellowship is from a Greek word and it's not used so much any more. We don't often say we are going to a ball game or to the movies to have fellowship. Fellowship means companionship and camaraderie with those who share our beliefs.

Refreshment is a word we use and recognise and although in The Salvation Army we think of refreshments as food and drink, it is much more. It means being uplifted, finding a new outlook, receiving strength, rest and relaxation. Thus the word 'fellowsment'…a blend of fellowship and refreshment. Stephen had coined a new word.

Perhaps John might have used it if it had been available to him. The three letters that John wrote had a specific purpose. John was a young man when he met Jesus face to face. He was called 'John the Beloved' and he was devoted to Jesus. John grew old.

Our granddaughter thinks when you are old, you are sick and weak! I once told her I was getting old and she asked her mother, 'Is my Gramie old?' Getting old happens to all of us and it makes us think about what is really important in life. John knew he would soon be 'promoted to Glory' and the cause of Christ would go on. However, his drive and aim to write these three letters was to proclaim the truth. 'Then you will know the truth, and the truth will set you free' (John 8:32).

John wants the followers of Christ to know and experience real joy. He is writing for his contemporaries, his generation. John realises that the gospel, the good news, has been infiltrated with some misconceptions such as the heresy of Gnosticism. Those who were 'adding to' and 'taking from' the truth were dangerously wrong. I wonder if it still happens today?

John writes the truth. Without the truth there could be no joy, no real fellowship or refreshment for the soul. In these first four verses of 1 John chapter one, we are included. God never intended his people to live lonely, isolated lives. John wants us to know that Jesus is God and he writes for our generation and generations to come. God has provided for our salvation and our joy comes from him.

We can find 'fellowsment' with a living God and with his people. Fellowship and refreshment will enable us to live like Jesus and to spread the good news.

Fellowship

Jesus is God – it is amazing, beyond understanding that you and I can have fellowship with the eternal God!

I am a soldier in The Salvation Army. I am a part of the worldwide Army. I know the General, but I have never had tea in her kitchen. I am an American. I pay taxes, pledge allegiance to the flag and I am proud of my country. However, I have never had dinner with the state governor or even been in the same room as the President.

And yet, John says we can have fellowship with the eternal God. We can have a relationship with Jesus. With that awesome privilege, with that unbelievable opportunity, let me ask you, what did you talk to him about this morning? How much of his word did you read? Maybe you were waiting, since you knew you would be in church this morning. So, will you pray this afternoon or spend time with him this evening? Perhaps you will remember to talk to him tonight before you close your eyes and trust him to keep you.

John proclaims Jesus as the 'Word of Life', who was from the beginning. There is no doubt, no maybe; Jesus is God. Let's say it together, 'Jesus is God!' Jesus was from the beginning. In Genesis 1:26, God spoke, 'Let us make mankind in our image'. God fellowshipped with man, walked with him in the cool of the evening. Sin destroyed the relationship of God with man: 'When the fullness of time was come, God sent forth his son' (Galatians 4:4 *KJV*). Jesus came to restore the fellowship man had with God. Jesus now intercedes for us and we can have fellowship with God.

Jesus is real – John says that he knew Jesus. He saw his face and looked into his eyes. He heard his voice and listened as he would teach, encourage and pray. John touched Jesus. He felt and experienced his presence. John found forgiveness, healing, purpose and love.

We too can experience the presence of Jesus. We can listen to his leading. We can see him through his word. We too can find forgiveness, healing, purpose and love. We can experience fellowship with God.

Fellowship is having companionship with those who are like-minded. It is sharing a purpose. Fellowship is being able to encourage each other in Christ. Finding strength, sharing sorrows and experiencing the joy that John is speaking of is vital for all of us. We need each other. True Christian fellowship is more than the casual greeting of the day or the famous 'see you next week'. Where is the fellowship from Monday through to Saturday? Why, when we are living on the edge and we need a friend, do we see our church family only once a week? Fellowship is not the gossip of the day or the complaint of tomorrow.

Christian fellowship is unique. It is in Christian community where children find security, teens are not judged, adults are encouraged and seniors are accepted. Christian fellowship is the environment where God's people can grow.

Refreshment

Sharing food – when it comes to refreshments, I think The Salvation Army excels. We know how to make a meal, we know how to set a table and we also know how to include everyone.

Did you ever think about how many times Jesus ate and drank with people? Do you remember the celebrations, events and even one-on-one conversations Jesus had, and how often there were refreshments?

There were wedding feasts like the one in Cana where he performed his first miracle, picnics on the mountainside where he shared the Beatitudes and other sermons, meals with his good friends Mary and Martha, and the final supper he had with the disciples; all times of refreshment.

We read that when Jesus called Zacchaeus from the tree he went to his house. Did he have tea? Well, the Bible doesn't say so, but I think Zacchaeus must have offered him some kind of refreshment. It is good for God's people to come together and eat.

More than just food – refreshment is so vital for all of us but, beyond food, refreshment is finding newness for your spirit. If I were to ask you to provide a meal, or if I were to suggest that I was the least bit hungry or thirsty, you would come to my aid. If I were to clear my throat a few times I know one or two of you would get me a glass of water. If I were to tell you someone from the congregation was in need, many of you would immediately ask how you could help. Are you willing to share more than food? John says, 'We proclaim to you what we have seen and heard, so that you also may have fellowship with us. And our fellowship is with the Father and with his Son, Jesus Christ' (1 John 1:3).

'We proclaim…' now who do you suppose 'we' could be? 'We' are the like-minded Christians who experience fellowship and refreshment together. Refreshment with each other is sharing more than your bread. It is sharing your time, your thoughts and your willingness to be 'real' with each other. It is being able to expose your needs and be willing to receive help. It is being willing to listen and really care for others. Refreshment is coming together with believers and finding a safe place to confess our weaknesses and share our joys.

Jesus attended parties and was relational with all people. Time and time again he had personal encounters with people from every walk of life. He spent time with them and ministered to them. When you have a relationship with Jesus and you are in a community of believers who care and love each other, you will share Christ. It will be as natural as waking up in the morning. Fellowship and refreshment…fellowsment with Christ and each other is where John tells us joy will be found. So…come on, let's have fellowsment!

If you do not know Jesus as Saviour and friend, we want to introduce you to him.

He can free you from sin and give you a life worth living. So…come on, let's have fellowsment!

Most of us would jump at the opportunity to have breakfast with the General or dinner with the President. Yet, you can meet with our Almighty God and have fellowship with him right now, every day, but do we? So…come on, let's have fellowsment!

Jesus Christ is God! Jesus was born and lived on Earth to show us how to live. Jesus lives to forgive us and intercede for us. We can have a relationship with Jesus. We can know the Word of Life. We can live in this everyday world experiencing sorrow, broken dreams, abuse and still overcome in the power of Jesus. 'In the world you will have tribulation; but be of good cheer. I [Jesus] have overcome the world' (John 16:33 *NKJV*).

We can know the truth and be free from our sin and our self. John says you can experience unbelievable joy. So…come on let's have fellowsment!

Let's share Christ with our family, friends, neighbours and all who are without fellowship, refreshment…Christ! We say we are afraid to talk to our families and friends about Christ. Would we rather see them perish, go to Hell? Would we rather see them struggle through life, while we experience abundant life?

Jesus says, 'Come unto me!' Jesus gives us joy and he gives us power to share that joy without fear.

Major Sharon Clanfield
Australia Eastern Territory

Time to Shout

Joshua chapter 6

IN the movie *Braveheart*, Mel Gibson, who plays the character of William Wallace, delivers a speech that inspires the army of men so that together they respond with one voice – a thunderous shout of affirmation – to the challenge laid before them.

William Wallace reminds this army of men that they were to stand up and fight for their freedom, not run from it or allow the enemy before them to rob them of it.

Prior to this the weary men were ready to throw in the towel because the battle seemed lost, but then with their next breath they shout with such abandonment, assured that they will conquer their foe. It wasn't a scream or cry, rather a united shout that victory was theirs for the taking.

In Joshua chapter 6, we read the story of the Israelites who also found their voice and together with a mighty shout caused the walls of Jericho to crumble and fall.

Background

The Israelites faced the land that their forefathers had gazed on 40 years previously but had failed to claim. From that time that generation had lived in fear of this place and its people, and consequently never fully enjoyed the promises God had in store for them.

God had rescued them from Egypt. That deliverance was never meant to just free them from the hold of the enemy but also to bring them into the Promised Land – into the place of God's presence – to enjoy the full blessing of the Lord. Despite this freedom, they remained captives, still bound by failure and fear.

So here stands Joshua and the people of Israel at the walls of Jericho, 40 years later. They have crossed the Jordan River into the land God had promised them, and the first obstacle before them is Jericho. The tall, strong walls block their way to the Promised Land.

At the end of Joshua chapter 5 we note that the Israelites had crossed the River Jordan and camped at Gilgal on the plains of Jericho. They started to eat the fruit of this abundant land, but God didn't want them to settle for these meagre helpings. He had so much more in store for them and he wanted them as a nation to fully experience it. They were on the brink of something great if they wanted it – but the walls of Jericho stood in the way and had to come down.

Walls

Two mammoth walls set 15 feet apart surrounded Jericho. At each gate there were watchmen making the walls seem vast and daunting – they looked indestructible and they were in the way of what God had for his people. The Israelites were confronted with this mighty fortress and God didn't want them to ignore it. He wanted the walls to come down to enable the Jewish nation to experience the fullness of his presence and his promises. God wanted to demonstrate his glory and almighty power through the people of Israel.

The purpose of God's Church is to display the glory of God's name with a mighty shout. God has so much more in store for all of us. What are the walls that stand in the way for us? What's holding us back from all God has to offer? God wants us to do something about those walls and anything that hinders our relationship with him.

Let's look at the instructions God gave to the Israelites when they came up against the walls of Jericho, and see how they broke through to move into the place God had promised.

Time to stop talking

In Joshua 6:10 *NLT* we read, "'Do not shout; do not even talk,"

Joshua commanded. "Not a single word from any of you until I tell you... Then shout!'"

Talking detracts from God

The Ark of the Lord was in the centre of the people when they marched, and any talking would draw them away from God, who was to be glorified amongst them. They were told to stop talking so that God would be central, not them. Constant chatter as they walked around the walls would take away from the one who was to be honoured on the march. The silence emphasised the presence of God among them.

Talking feeds discouragement and fear

They were told not to talk so as to not speak words of discouragement or negativity that would hinder them as they faced the walls; not to speak words that would allow the spirit of fear to take a hold of them.

This was the problem with the generation before them, when God wanted to lead them into the Promised Land. Moses sent out 12 spies to check out the land and 10 of them returned and discouraged the people with their ill-chosen words and negativity, arousing fear within them and causing them to doubt that God would give them this land.

They were not ready to speak, let alone shout. Words are so important – marching around Jericho and speaking before the time was ripe would not bring the walls down.

This was a lesson in the importance of words. Careless words cannot be thrown away once spoken, but positive words have the ability to do great things when spoken at the right time.

Talking can hold up progress

We can sit around and talk about the walls for so long and never deal with them in the way God wants us to. God tells us to stop talking about it and start moving forward to claim what he is giving us.

Time to stop striving

They were given instructions to walk around the walls of Jericho for six days and on the seventh day to walk around seven times. The march around the city of Jericho wasn't to show them how hard they had to work, it was all about perseverance. History teaches us to strive to make it; God teaches us to do things in his strength. The march taught them they could never bring down those walls in their own strength; it was God alone who had the power to do this.

Build your faith

The circling of the walls was the means to build their faith in the God who said: 'I will give you this city'. We think our faith is strengthened when we face little things without God's help, but that only builds self-dependence. When we face walls that in our own strength we cannot penetrate, we have to depend on God alone to bring them down, and these are the walls God wants us to face to strengthen our faith in him.

Glimpse of something greater

God also used these walls to stir within his people a hunger for all he had to give. He gives us a glimpse of something beyond where we are and invites us to take a hold of it.

Time to start shouting

It's time to stop talking, it's time to stop striving, it's time to start shouting – God has given us the city. God wants his Army to find their shout.

We need to position ourselves together in a place to be a part of the Lord's mighty shout. It's time for a shout to go out from the Church that will cause people to stop and listen. A shout that will bring down the walls the enemy has put up to stop the army of God.

Army of God, it's time to shout! It's time for the walls to fall in your city, it's time for the walls to fall in your life, in your work, in your family, in your home, and it's time to move forward to possess all the land the Lord has to give us.

The enemy may seem intimidating but the truth is they are scared and defeated. Why do you think they were hiding behind the walls in the first place? The people of Jericho were afraid of the Lord's army; they had shut themselves away frightened of the God of Israel.

The enemy knows that he has no power over the Lord's mighty army. His only plan is to make us feel he is stronger than us and will use any walls he can to make us believe it.

What are those walls that need to come tumbling down for you? What are the walls that have held you back from all God has in store for you?

We need to find our shout – the shout is not a desperate cry for help, for God has already rescued us, rather it is a shout of faith in the God of miracles who has so much more for his people to claim.

It's a shout of recognition in the one and only God who is above all and who has done and will do immeasurably more than we could ever hope or imagine. It's a shout of confidence in our God and King. It's a shout of declaration that we belong to him and that he is our God. It's a shout of faith that God is true to all his promises. It's a shout of joy because he gives victory.

Psalm 100:1 *NLT* exhorts us to, 'Shout with joy to the Lord, all the Earth!' Psalm 66:1 *NLT* says, 'Shout joyful praises to God, all the Earth!' and verse four says, 'Shouting your name in glorious songs'.

It's time to take the land God has promised us with a mighty shout!

- Shout and the borders are enlarged
- Shout and the enemy will lose his ground
- Shout and the walls that hold you back will come down
- Shout because God has given you this city

It is time for the world to hear The Salvation Army, God's army, shout – in a world of desperate need we have something to shout about.

- God has delivered us
- God has given us victory
- God has blessed us
- God has saved us
- God has shown us his love and mercy

- God has set us free
- God has made us in his image

We are in a season of 'shout'. God has given us this city – let the city hear the shout of the Lord's army among them and see our boundaries extended and the enemy defeated and lives won to the Kingdom of God.

- Army, are you ready to shout?
- Are you ready for all God has to give you?
- Are you ready to see those walls that have held you back crumble to the ground?
- Are you ready to move into that intimate place of God's fullness and presence?

It is time to open your mouth and shout the name of Jesus. It is time to face the walls in your life and shout out the name of Jesus and bring them down. Together as loud as we can, let us shout to the Lord with a voice of triumph, let us lift his name with a mighty shout of faith!

Captain Jenny Collings
New Zealand, Fiji and Tonga Territory

Total Freedom
John 15:9-11

IF anyone had heard the screams of little Carolina Anderson on that sunny day in January 2003, I'm sure they would be etched on the listener's mind for all time.

Seven-year-old Carolina was viciously attacked by a dog while playing in a park in Auckland, New Zealand. It was reported that the injuries to her face were so severe that her appearance was unrecognisable. She lost an eye and endured 10 hours of surgery in the first instance, followed by multiple reconstructive surgeries, with still more to follow. This attack, along with a spate of others, became the catalyst for New Zealand's dog control laws to be overhauled.

Seven years later there was a call from dog owners and sympathetic politicians to see these laws (which had been tightened) relaxed. A leading politician, Hon. Rodney Hide, endorsed a review of dog laws that, in his words, would 'ensure the emphasis is on freedom rather than restriction'. Imagine the outcry from those who have suffered from living under a flawed system in the past! People like Carolina, her parents and other supporters were outraged at such a move. If politicians and dog owners alike achieve the freedom they want, then the freedom of others to play and go out for walks, without the risk of being viciously attacked by a dog, is at risk.

As I think about all the facets of an issue like this, my mind is drawn back to when I was studying Law at university. One of my favourite classes was Civil Liberties. We would spend hours discussing human rights and the individual's right to be free – free to make his/her own choices and to live a healthy and happy life. We would fiercely debate to what extent one person's freedom should be allowed to infringe upon another's.

I remember the lecturer asking questions like: 'Should people be free to do whatever they choose?' The majority would answer a resounding 'Yes!' The fact that they were all students, thoroughly enjoying their newfound freedom and experimental lifestyles, undoubtedly influenced their stance! I, however, was in the minority.

My response to them went something like this: 'Hang on a minute; what you're saying will backfire. One person's decision to do whatever they like will eventually affect another's values or choices in an adverse way. If we are going to live together in communities then we have to agree on some core values that protect the freedom we have to make our own choices, at the same time as respecting others.'

So, the question that arises for me from all of this is, 'What is true freedom?' Is true freedom found in being able to do whatever we like; whatever we think will make us happy? Or is it found through the acceptance of some essential, mutually agreed core values?

I would argue that it is the latter. If humanity is to be free, then we need to discover and come to an acceptance of some essential core values that will allow us to live together peacefully.

The Ten Commandments, found in Exodus 20:1-17, are an example of such values. They are foundational standards that, if mutually accepted and obeyed, go a long way in allowing humans to live peacefully together.

Is it possible that freedom can be found in following laws? Think about our everyday lives. If you fail to follow the law, there is a good chance that your freedom will end up being restricted, as breaking the law can lead to imprisonment. It is the same with spiritual freedom. Disobedience to God's laws, to his model for living, leads to spiritual imprisonment. Acceptance of God's core values, as expressed in the Bible, leads to spiritual freedom.

So, let me ask you this: Are you experiencing spiritual freedom today? To know true spiritual freedom, you must discover God's core values. This takes place when we put our trust in Jesus Christ, the one who came to

50

show us how to live at peace with God and with each other. Jesus is the only one who has the power to free us from captivity. He is the one who has come to release us from imprisonment and rescue us from danger.

Here is an example of Jesus calling his followers to trust in him. 'Now it happened, on a certain day, that he got into a boat with his disciples. And he said to them, "Let us cross over to the other side of the lake." And they launched out. But as they sailed he fell asleep. And a windstorm came down on the lake, and they were filling with water, and were in jeopardy. And they came to him and awoke him, saying, "Master, Master, we are perishing!" Then he arose and rebuked the wind and the raging of the water. And they ceased, and there was a calm. But he said to them, "Where is your faith?" And they were afraid, and marvelled, saying to one another, "Who can this be? For he commands even the winds and water, and they obey him!"' (Luke 8:22-25 NKJV).

A powerful picture of trust! It says to us today that we must trust that Jesus is the one who has the power, capacity and desire to save us from the enemy. It is not enough just to know about Jesus by reading the Scriptures, you need to believe and accept that he is your rescuer and invite him as a person to come into your life and free you completely.

Listen to these words of Jesus, 'You search the Scriptures, for in them you think you have eternal life; and these are they which testify of me. But you are not willing to come to me that you may have life' (John 5:39-40 NKJV).

In other words, it's not just enough to know about him, you must get to know Jesus personally by receiving him into your life. How do you do that? The Bible tells us, 'If you confess with your mouth the Lord Jesus and believe in your heart that God has raised him from the dead, you will be saved. For with the heart one believes unto righteousness, and with the mouth confession is made unto salvation. For the Scripture says, "Whoever believes on him will not be put to shame." For there is no distinction between Jew and Greek, for the same Lord over all is rich to all who call upon him. For "whoever calls on the name of the Lord shall be saved"' (Romans 10:9-13 NKJV).

The apostle Paul wrote these words. He started out in life with the philosophy that the law alone would save him. He went on to discover in a dramatic conversion experience that it was the person of Jesus Christ who embodied and fulfilled the law. Jesus, who held the power to give Paul true freedom, came to rescue him and save his life. Even though Paul had met Jesus on the road to Damascus, his spiritual freedom was not complete until he had been filled with the Holy Spirit. We are told in Acts chapter nine, 'And Ananias went his way and entered the house; and laying hands on him he said, "Brother Saul, the Lord Jesus, who appeared to you on the road as you came, has sent me that you may receive your sight and be filled with the Holy Spirit"' (Acts 9:17 *NKJV*).

It is the same with us. We may have been introduced to Jesus and even believed that he is Lord, but until we submit ourselves entirely to the indwelling of the Holy Spirit we will not experience the real freedom that comes from full salvation.

What about once we've got that freedom? How do we keep it? We need to make sure that we stay with the one who gave us freedom. With Jesus there is safety and security. With Jesus there is protection from evil. With spiritual obedience there is spiritual freedom.

'As the Father loved me, I also have loved you; abide in my love. If you keep my commandments, you will abide in my love, just as I have kept my Father's commandments and abide in his love. These things I have spoken to you, that my joy may remain in you, and that your joy may be full' (John 15:9-11 *NKJV*).

This passage of Scripture is a picture of the integral link between spiritual obedience and spiritual freedom. They go hand in hand and are all played out in the context of God's great love for us and our response of loving obedience to him.

When a Christian chooses to go outside God's will for them, outside his commandments, there will be deep-seated spiritual struggle in their lives. A peace they had known in times of being right with God will be disturbed and there will be spiritual confusion and conflict.

Think of it like this. There are times when the freedoms of an individual, a community or a nation are impinged on through invasion. This is the case during wartime. One army invades another's territory with the aim of capturing it. The same kind of invasion happens on a spiritual level as well. 'For we do not wrestle against flesh and blood, but against principalities, against powers, against the rulers of the darkness of this age, against spiritual hosts of wickedness in the heavenly places' (Ephesians 6:12 *NKJV*).

The enemy invades and claims territory for his own and we must resist him. He is intent on destruction and will use every power at his disposal to bind up souls with evils such as anger, hatred, fear, bitterness, jealousy, deceit, despair and self-sufficiency. When we succumb to enemy invasion, a battle of wills results; where once we had fully surrendered to God, now we are taking back control, piece by piece. With each choice to go outside of the Lord's will, God is gradually edged out to the sidelines of our lives.

We need to make sure that we daily dress in the armour that God supplies to his soldiers. To paraphrase Ephesians 6:13-20, 'Put on your belt of truth, the breastplate of righteousness and the shoes of the gospel of peace. Take up the shield of faith, put on the helmet of salvation and use the sword of the Spirit.'

Without our armour on, we leave ourselves completely open to be invaded or captured by the enemy. Perhaps, right now, your guard is down; you've become lazy and complacent in your walk with Jesus. Do you realise that by choosing that approach to your faith, you are in effect spiritually vulnerable and can be taken over by enemy forces in a matter of moments? Put your armour on so that you will be able to stand firm against the enemy and be used by God to rescue others in danger.

There are some who live daily in enemy territory and struggle to reach safety. Their lives are spent in the constant clutches of evil. These people need to be rescued. They need brave soldiers who will go and fight for their freedom and offer them a way out. Salvationists have a calling and a mandate to go into the world and rescue those who are drowning in sin and darkness. You have a part to play in that work. If you know the reality of true freedom in Jesus, don't you want the same for others? I do! What a difference it would make to this world if those who know and experience true God-given freedom shared that good news with those who are lost, bound and hurting.

True freedom for each of us is found in acknowledging God as the ultimate freedom-keeper and peacemaker and submitting entirely to his cause. True freedom is found in accepting God's call to join Christ's fight, in the power of the Holy Spirit, to see every person being saved from the enemy and spiritually free. True freedom is found in full submission to God. As the Scriptures remind us, 'Therefore submit to God. Resist the devil and he will flee from you' (James 4:7 *NKJV*).

How do you fully submit to God? You submit by dying to self. You need to hand over your will, your desires, your dreams, your wants, your life, entirely into the hands of the living God and continually trust him. You need to give over complete control of your life to God.

'For me, to live is Christ, and to die is gain' (Philippians 1:21 *NKJV*). When we accept Christ and die to self we gain everything because we gain the Spirit of God living within us, bringing freedom and fullness of life like we have never known. Christ is the living water. The Spirit of Christ within is an eternal spring that never runs dry of spiritual refreshment and resource. He fills and empowers us to overflowing when we let him! Have you experienced that? Do you know what it is to have the Spirit of the living God dwell within you and constantly water your soul? Everything is different when this happens to you. You can never be the same again. If you let him, God will gift you with a deep experience of his supernatural power and love that will change your life forever. Because once you know his indwelling you will not want to live life without him.

Do you want this? Then seek God now. Call out to your rescuer. Kneel before him asking him to save you. Place your life entirely in God's hands. He is the only one worth trusting with that responsibility. Give the Spirit of Christ full control today and experience total freedom.

Major Lesa Davis
USA Central Territory

Faith or Forgery?

James 1:2-4

Consider it pure joy, my brothers and sisters, whenever you face trials of many kinds, because you know that the testing of your faith produces perseverance. Let perseverance finish its work so that you may be mature and complete, not lacking anything.

Introduction

THERE is an American television show called *Antiques Roadshow* that has been popular for many years. At first glance it doesn't seem all that interesting. A team of appraisers travels around the country, stopping in various cities to meet people and assess the value of their antiques. There are no car chases, love stories or medical dramas involved. But there is always an element of mystery – what is each treasured object really worth?

Occasionally, someone presents an object – a chair or a painting, maybe – and the appraiser informs them that the item they thought was a priceless antique isn't actually worth anything because it's a forgery. The eyes of a trained expert expose all the little clues that a casual observer might miss. Because they know what to look for, the appraisers can detect fake ageing techniques, machine-made parts and artificial finishes. The treasured chair that supposedly came from the home of one of America's founding fathers sometimes turns out to be a factory-made replica hardly older than the person presenting it. In a few cases, the frame around a painting has turned out be more valuable than the fake painting inside. A quick series of tests can expose a fake treasure.

The book of James is a bit like a training manual for spiritual assessment or appraisal. Through a series of examples, James asks his readers to look at their life of faith and determine whether it is authentic (priceless because it is the gift of God purchased by the blood of Jesus) or a forgery (worthless because it is only self-made). The first chapter of James focuses on three areas that can expose a fake faith. We can varnish over our spiritual life with all kinds of faux finishes, but these three questions are good starting places for determining the authenticity of our faith:

1.   How does our faith react to trials and temptations? (vv 2-18)
2.   How does our faith practise what is preached? (vv 19-21)
3.   How does our faith affect the people around us? (vv 26-27)

Trials and temptations expose authentic faith

'Consider it a sheer gift, friends, when tests and challenges come at you from all sides. You know that under pressure, your faith-life is forced into the open and shows its true colours' (James 1:2 *TM*).

James wrote his letter to a church facing many problems, including divisiveness, intolerance, favouritism and inequalities among the members. False teachers were leading believers astray. The community of faith was growing, but also splintering and spreading around the Roman Empire and the world. New converts – with all their personal and cultural biases – were being added to the small original group. Church leaders and members had plenty of challenges to deal with, including persecution from threatened government officials.

To them and to us, James says that trials and temptations are gifts. They are meant to produce a response of joy because they are opportunities where God can transform and refine us. James is not talking about some kind of positive-thinking programme. He is acknowledging that believers like us will face all kinds of hard situations. Those situations will test the very essence of our faith at times.

When I think of this, I remember Dave, a member of our congregation several years ago. Dave had been almost destroyed by alcohol. He came to the Lord reluctantly, almost as a last resort. His faith was simple and hesitant. He was sorely tempted to return to his life of alcoholism and petty crime. But somehow he managed to hold on to his simple faith that God would save and help him. We had the great privilege of seeing the transformation from Dave-the-alcoholic to Dave-the-follower-of-Jesus. Those struggles to stay sober, to rebuild broken relationships and to learn to live as a transformed individual became sources of great joy, not only for Dave but also the whole congregation as we watched him grow and mature.

That is what James was talking about. Our faith struggles force us to the place where we ask God for wisdom (v 5) and that allows us to endure until we are moulded more and more into his image. When we ask God for help, his response is always generous! Faith itself is a gift from God, but he doesn't stop there. He continues to give us everything we need to live godly lives in this world.

Human interactions – especially the challenging ones – expose authentic faith

'My dear brothers and sisters, take note of this: everyone should be quick to listen, slow to speak and slow to become angry, because human anger does not produce the righteousness that God desires. Therefore, get rid of all moral filth and the evil that is so prevalent, and humbly accept the word planted in you, which can save you' (vv 19-21).

The question is, what will happen when your faith is challenged to show its true colours? If that's not a big enough question for you, try this one: How often does your speech expose the truth about your faith?

Let's face it, people are often part of those trials and temptations we just talked about! Even in the church – maybe especially in the church – your relationships with the people around you say an awful lot about the state of your relationship with God. Maybe that is why James goes right for the throat, or more accurately, for the mouth when he writes, '…be quick to listen, slow to speak and slow to become angry' (v 19).

Most of us would admit that we have had more than one problem with anger and our mouths. Harsh words, intemperate conversations and/or gossip can ruin relationships, and even whole congregations, when they go unchecked.

Even if we're not guilty of malicious gossip, our mouths can expose our immature faith in more subtle ways. In her book *Move Over Victoria – I Know the Real Secret*, Christian author Nancy Kennedy humorously captures the problem. 'I supposed I should warn you: if you ever meet me in person and we have a conversation, be prepared to have only the second to last word because I have the last word. Always. (That's because I'm right.)' She continues, 'Also be prepared to have me correct you when you're wrong. It's just a little public service gesture I like to offer. But don't worry. I'm so good at it, you will hardly notice I'm tearing you down (or at least adding to your limited knowledge on a subject) in order to build myself up.'

Her words are clearly tongue-in-cheek, but the reality is that we all struggle with maintaining control over our emotions and controlling our tongues. That is why James goes on to urge his readers to 'humbly accept the word planted in you, which can save you' (v 21) and 'look intently into the perfect law that gives freedom' (v 25). Our own efforts will never be enough. Instead, we humbly nurture the life of Christ in us and let his word take root in hearts softened by worship, much like a gardener cares not just for the plant but for the soil itself so that the plant's roots can go down deep and provide health from the inside out.

Destructive anger and uncontrolled speech come from hard hearts. Authentic faith softens our hearts toward God and consequently to the people around us – especially the people who are most likely to be exploited.

The way we treat vulnerable people exposes authentic faith

'Religion that God our Father accepts as pure and faultless is this: to look after orphans and widows in their distress and to keep oneself from being polluted by the world' (v 27).

God shows special concern for people on the bottom rungs of society's ladder. Throughout the Old Testament, caring for widows and orphans (those who are most helpless and vulnerable) is a major theme. God is shown as the defender of the fatherless and poor. He urges the nation of Israel to care for the outsiders living among them.

When the mother of James and John approached Jesus to ask that her sons be given special honour in his Kingdom (Matthew 20:20-28), the rest of the disciples were understandably upset. Jesus stopped the argument by reminding them that the rulers of the Gentiles and others lord it over those under them, but he is emphatic in his words to them, 'Not so with you. Instead, whoever wants to become great among you must be your servant, and whoever wants to be first must be your slave – just as the Son of Man did not come to be served, but to serve, and to give his life as a ransom for many' (Matthew 20:26-28).

If you want to be great, learn to serve. And whom should we serve? If the answer wasn't clear enough, Jesus went on to tell the disciples a parable (Matthew 25:31-46) about the time when the Son of Man comes in glory and separates the righteous (sheep) from the unrighteous (goats). He describes the righteous as feeding him when he was hungry, clothing him when he was needy and visiting him when he was sick or even in prison. When they protest that they don't remember doing those things for him, he replies, 'Truly I tell you, whatever you did for one of the least of these brothers and sisters of mine, you did for me' (Matthew 25:40).

The essential spirit of this world is self-indulgence at all costs. We could very well go through life caring only for ourselves. It is very easy to ignore the homeless, the mentally ill, the disenfranchised, the exploited people on the fringes of society. But James reminds us that pure religion embraces them. The way we treat the at-risk people around us exposes the true state of our faith.

Conclusion

Imagine that you are queuing at the 'Faith Roadshow'. Your faith is waiting for an appraisal by the ultimate appraiser of the universe. What will be the verdict – faith or forgery?

Major Marlene George
Canada and Bermuda Territory

Broken Dolls Restored

Mark 5:25-34

IF there is one kind of toy that has been a playtime favourite for little girls throughout the world and across the generations it would have to be, without a doubt, dolls!

Most little girls have their favourite doll and I had mine. My Uncle Hedley gave her to me when I was six years old. She was a beautiful baby doll dressed in a lacy white christening gown. She had blonde hair and blue glass eyes that closed when you laid her down and opened when you picked her up. She was almost too beautiful to take out of the box but, being a typical six-year-old, I begged to play with her. Over the next months and years, I continued to play with her...in fact you might say I played the stuffing out of her! By the time she was finally discarded some 10 years later, she looked nothing like she did when I received her. She had little hair left, few eyelashes, and one of her eyes wouldn't open and close anymore. The stitching around her arms and legs was giving way – you can picture it, can't you? After many hours of wear and tear in the hands of a busy child at play, my once perfectly beautiful baby doll was now badly broken, fit only to be thrown away. What a sad tale – the story of a broken doll.

In my years as a social worker and Salvation Army officer I have encountered many broken dolls. Living dolls (both male and female), once beautiful, who have been tattered and torn by the abrasiveness of life like broken dolls that society has discarded. Yet the good news of the Bible is a message of hope for brokenness; it is a message that speaks hope and life

61

into dead and dry bones; it is a message that clearly calls all to healing and wholeness through the grace of Jesus Christ.

Allow me to share the stories of a few 'broken dolls' found in Scripture, with the hope that their story and the news of their restoration and healing will be a source of encouragement to you.

Naomi: broken by grief

In Ruth chapter one we are introduced to a woman named Naomi. Through a famine in the land, Naomi's husband Elimelek took his wife and two sons from Bethlehem and relocated in the country of Moab. It was while living there that Naomi's life began to fall apart. In verses three and four we read the reason for her brokenness; 'Now Elimelek, Naomi's husband, died, and she was left with her two sons. They married Moabite women, one named Orpah and the other Ruth. After they had lived there about 10 years, both Mahlon and Kilion also died, and Naomi was left without her two sons and her husband.'

Here is a woman, probably middle-aged, living in a foreign land, away from family and friends who, within 10 years, finds herself widowed and childless, left seemingly alone in her world – a broken doll.

Anyone who has known the pain of losing a loved one can relate to the brokenness of grief. Some have described this experience as feeling like you are missing a limb from your body. Your right hand (person) has been torn away and you feel the pain and brokenness of that separation. Grief counsellors have suggested that there is no greater grief than that of losing a child – Naomi lost her two children *and* her husband through death, which resulted in her brokenness of spirit.

Those who are grieving will attest that often healing comes through sharing their grief with another. If you continue to read the book of Ruth, there is a beautiful story of how God's hand was on Naomi. God provided for her and her young daughter-in-law, Ruth, who would not leave her, but faithfully cared for her as they supported one another through the pain of grief. Naomi made a declaration to return to her homeland and Ruth returned with her. In time, Ruth met Boaz who was related to Naomi's husband and, according to Jewish custom, the rightful marriage partner for Ruth. For Naomi, who had experienced a winter of desolation, spring arrived and she was able to enjoy a new season in her life. The family Naomi thought she had seen perish would be restored in the genealogies of Israel. The son of Ruth and Boaz was Obed, the grandfather of King David, who was the greatest king of Israel.

Naomi, a broken doll, broken by the pain of grief, was not cast aside, or discarded by her Creator, but restored; '…in all things God works for the good of those who love him…' (Romans 8:28). In time, by God's grace, Naomi could sing this new song, 'He's turned my mourning into dancing, he's turned my sorrow into joy, a song of praise instead of sadness…and for my tears the oil of joy.'

Perhaps someone who is reading this sermon has been drowning in a violent sea of grief because of some significant loss in your life; be it through death, separation or divorce, and you feel like you're going down for the last time. Can I encourage you through the word of God with the words, 'I will never leave you nor forsake you' (Joshua 1:5).

The woman broken by illness

In three of the gospels, Matthew 9:20-22, Mark 5:25-34, and Luke 8:43-48, we have the record of a woman who had endured an illness, which rendered her legally unclean, for more than 12 years. She could not openly throw herself at the feet of Christ and state her complaint because legally she was not permitted to be out in public. Somehow her approach would have to go unnoticed by the crowd, yet her faith assured her if she could only touch the hem of his garment, she would be cured and her brokenness healed!

We can only imagine what this woman had endured at the hands of the medical men of that day for we are told that she 'had suffered many things from many physicians…and was no better, but rather grew worse' (*NKJV*). Yet where men had failed, Christ succeeded. What is not possible with men is blessedly possible with God. The woman had suffered for more than 12 years, yet she was instantly healed as soon as she touched the hem of Christ's garment! She might have stayed in her dark corner, but found the courage to bring her brokenness to the Great Physician and so her brokenness was no more. She was restored. Jesus said to her, 'Daughter, your faith has healed you. Go in peace.'

As you read this sermon can you identify with this once broken doll? Perhaps you too have 'suffered many things from many physicians' and you are saying, 'If I could touch the hem of his garment, if I could only touch one part of his robe, I know I'd be healed and my sins would be forgiven.'

The Great Physician, the sympathising Jesus, is still in the business of healing even now. In the present century, God continues to place his healing hand on broken bodies and restores them to health.

The woman at the well: broken by sin

We read the famous encounter of the Samaritan woman with Jesus in John chapter four. Jesus is sitting by the town well waiting for his disciples to return from Samaria with some food. In the heat of the day, on her own – because she was a social outcast in her town – a woman came to fill her water pots and there, at the well, her life was changed forever!

The woman of Samaria represents many others on the pages of Scripture who, like her, were broken dolls – broken by the sin of adultery. We think of Bathsheba, Gomer, Rahab, 'slaves to the flesh', giving or selling their bodies to the 'highest bidder' and all the time straying from God's intention for them.

In my many years of counselling I have learned that the root of this brokenness is sometimes due to choices that were the result of being victims of abuse and/or neglect during childhood years. It is often unresolved pain and brokenness that has subsequently driven individuals like the Samaritan woman to spend a lifetime searching for true love and acceptance, only to find herself looking for love in all the wrong places.

Jesus' approach to this woman was a classic example of the best of Christian evangelism. Jesus proceeded gently and showed this woman more respect in one conversation than she had known in her whole lifetime. In this healing encounter Jesus empathetically revealed both the truth of who he was and his life-changing message of amazing grace! Amazing grace – as, by the Holy Spirit, the woman acknowledged her belief in Christ and immediately became a powerful witness to others, sharing her remarkable discovery.

This broken doll was restored by a spiritual heart transplant right there at Jacob's well! The woman who avoided the crowds because of her shame now rushed back to the city to tell everyone about her new-found faith in Christ, 'Come, see a man, which told me all things that ever I did: is not this the Christ?' (John 4:29 *KJV*). Jesus restored this broken doll and awakened her to a new and better life. 'If any man be in Christ, he is a new creature: old things are passed away; behold, all things become new' (2 Corinthians 5:17 *KJV*).

Without doubt, this list could go on and on – broken dolls restored by the amazing grace of the Lord Jesus Christ. Written on the pages of history are multitudes of biblical and contemporary accounts of broken dolls – women (and men) broken emotionally by grief, broken physically by illness, broken emotionally and spiritually by sin – being restored and lives being changed forever.

Isn't it wonderful that the same Jesus who ministered emotional, physical, mental and spiritual healing in the past continues his ministry of restoration and healing even today?

The essence of this message is captured in a favourite 'Treasured Memories' ornament. The one called 'Dolly's Doctor' is a model of a little girl bringing her doll to her daddy to fix for her. I think this ornament serves as a picture of what God our heavenly Father desires for each one of us – that we bring our brokenness to him to heal and restore. For in Heaven's eyes there are no losers, no hopeless cases. God has a blessing for you!

Major Ronda Gilger
USA Western Territory

The Healing of
the Paralysed Man
Mark 2:1-12

WE are invited into the story! Let us try to read Scripture narratives in such a way that we 'see' what the author is trying to reveal, peeling back the layers of truth one at a time. It's a process of discovery of who God is and who we are in light of the kind of God he is.

As we look at Mark 2:1-12 we are personally invited to sit front row centre, to see the wonder upon the paralytic's face as he takes his first steps as a whole, healed man; to hear Jesus' words; to experience the struggle, the conflicts and the richness of the story as a part of the complete story of God and his loved people.

Jesus is returning from the Galilean region to Capernaum (v 1) which many scholars refer to as being Jesus' 'own town', his home base (Matthew 9:1). Excavations of ancient Capernaum (situated by the Sea of Galilee) give us exciting clues about this seaside city characterised by urban 'townhouses' with small roofed rooms clustered around large courtyards; allowing us to almost visualise the setting where the crowds pressed in to see and hear Jesus. Among the artefacts found were remains of homes, water systems, fish markets, mooring docks, pottery from the Roman occupation era, and large sections of urban housing.

I am fascinated by archaeology, delighting as history confirms the truth of God's Word! I can imagine the smells of the sea, the sights, and

67

hillsides covered in first century town homes and the enclosed courtyard where Jesus taught.

The story of the healing of the paralytic is comprised primarily of Jesus' spoken words, which draw a crowd and provoke wonder, suspicion, anger and amazement. Other characters actually have very little to say and it is fascinating to think that we can extract most of their words from this story without affecting the central message. Their thoughts and actions speak much louder than their words!

The people who make up the crowd are 'the curious'; they form the backdrop for the main scene. When they are amazed and praise God, saying, 'We have never seen anything like this!' (v 12), they have not comprehended spiritually what they have seen with their physical eyes. They are those desperately seeking hope, yet missing God standing right there with them.

The paralytic and his four friends have arrived late, but will allow neither the crowd nor the roof to hinder them in their quest to reach Jesus. There are no words spoken and yet Jesus perceives their great faith manifested as action. They will not allow any obstacle to stop them (v 4). Their presence is also very important to the story because their boldness creates another 'sub-theme' in which the religious teachers' private thoughts emerge as they wrestle with the identity of Christ (vv 6-7). The plot thickens! Their sceptical scholars' discussion becomes the launching pad from which Jesus' message springs (vv 8-10). And I would not be surprised if we find ourselves identifying with the characters in matters of truth, need, faith and healing.

What kind of faith is this?

The paralysed man's friends have gone to extraordinary measures to place him in front of Jesus. This active faith becomes the basis for the healing (v 5). In this passage faith is interpreted as 'complete confidence in someone' as in a court trial where your future lies solely in the hands of the judge. This level of faithfulness has an element of desperation. While there are some who might suggest that faith is a quiet, confident trust that gives resolve and hope, in this narrative it shows itself as a radically alive, action-packed faith; the type needed to step forward to integrate the proclamation that Jesus makes about himself (v 10) and his Kingdom. This is faith that has moved from the sidelines to centre court.

Incredible firsts you won't want to miss!

Mark 2:1 begins by giving us some information, 'A few days later' implying that the event we are looking at comes after another that lends to our understanding. If you began reading Mark at chapter two you have already come in late for the performance of Mark's drama. We can read about those who are forgiven, amazed, healed and wonder 'Who is this Jesus?', but if we have not read Mark chapter one we do not understand that he is indeed the Son of the divine voice in whom the Spirit is at work. There are moments of glory in this first chapter and as we move into Mark 2:1-12 we see some very important 'firsts', foreshadowing what lies ahead.

Mark's Gospel is the first written, chronologically. Mark is presenting the Son of God/Son of Man, giving evidence as to who he is – and he is doing it 'on the record'. We are invited into this story and observe that, as the paralytic is lowered through the ceiling, Jesus stops teaching and directs his undivided attention towards these who have created a social disturbance, not to mention the huge mess in the host's home (v 4). Instead of chastising them for causing such disorder, Jesus does the unexpected; supernaturally 'seeing' their faith, he imparts spiritual wholeness ('Son, your sins are forgiven' [v 5]).

This is the first record of Jesus' ability to perceive the condition of the soul of those he encounters. This particular use of the word 'see' ('eido' in Greek) is used often at the beginning of a story to draw attention to, or to advertise, something. It lets the reader know that something of great importance is at hand. In this case the reader should note that what is to be 'seen' goes way beyond the ordinary. This is extraordinary sight or 'seeing'. There is a shift from sensory seeing to an awareness where things become crystal clear. Jesus sees past the obvious need of physical healing and does what is of greatest eternal significance in light of the Kingdom of God, hence the next 'first'; that of pronouncing forgiveness.

Another 'first' in this passage occurs in verse eight, as Jesus knows immediately what the teachers of the law are thinking. This is not an example of extrasensory perception, but of divine perception, Jesus having the mind of God and yet being fully human; this becomes a pivotal issue for the spiritually myopic religious leaders present.

As readers of this story, we are learning these 'firsts' about the Kingdom of God as well. We can see that there is a great contrast between those who possess great minds who cannot perceive; and the lowly, the shunned, the unclean, who possess a simple faith. If you are especially watchful you might also perceive the silent lesson about who is preferred in the Kingdom of God.

It is in this passage that we hear Jesus' first pronouncement that he is the Son of Man (v 10). Intertwined with his title is our fifth 'first' in Mark 2:1-12 as we see that the 'Son of Man' has been granted God's exclusive authority (v 10) to forgive. Because God forgives the paralytic, Jesus can heal him. Astounding!

Sceptics on the sidelines

Jesus' statement that he had authority to forgive sins is central to this story. This announcement bordered on blasphemy, a capital crime, of which the religious leaders were very aware. To make such a statement was audacious, but to back it up was quite another thing! Jesus was not accused of saying that he was God, but of doing what only God can do (e.g. Isaiah 43:25, 44:22). While these religious leaders understood that they could appeal to God on behalf of the guilty, they actually did read the Scripture correctly as saying that God alone could forgive. Jesus left these leaders to unravel the identity of 'the Son of Man' for themselves with his open-ended answer, 'Who can forgive sins but *God* alone?' (v 7).

After Jesus addresses the scribes he turns to the paralytic with a direct command, 'I tell you, get up, take your mat and go home.' The paralytic does not hesitate. He obeys, immediately, and goes home forgiven, and healed (vv 11-12). He has heard, and acted from a heart of absolute faith and trust in the Son of Man. Quite a contrast in behaviour from the teachers! This story could have had quite another ending had the paralytic been sceptical, couldn't it?

Who is Jesus?

Jesus allows us to see his identity today in the same way as if we had been present in that room when the paralytic was lowered from the hole in the ceiling by his friends. Through these verses we have the opportunity to come to terms with what it means that Jesus is fully God and fully man. We are also now aware of the kind of faith of Christ's followers in the Kingdom of God. That the Son of Man has authority to forgive and to heal should generate awe within our hearts, for the Jesus of today is this same Son of Man revealed in Mark 2:1-12.

'God came among us in a unique and powerful way, showing us a new kind of life and giving each of us a new vision for our life together, and for the world we live in. Jesus is more compelling than ever. More inviting, more true, more mysterious than ever!' – Rob Bell, *Velvet Elvis: Repainting the Christian Faith*.

Jesus is also presented as the healer, not only of the paralytic of first century Capernaum, but for those of us who are paralysed, suffering from an inability to move, whether that be generated from our own fears, circumstances, finances or physical health. He is the only one who truly knows what we face each day and our heart's longing for him. Having been granted the authority to forgive, the Son of Man knows that our greatest need is for wholeness and healing of our souls. He is not shocked by our thoughts, appearance, or our past.

Each human is allowed the freedom to struggle with his or her own destiny through personal words and acts. Daily, we are given opportunities to exercise faith in ways that beckon Heaven to touch us where we are, to enter into the Kingdom of God. Each of us is allowed, as was the crowd on that day so long ago, to 'see', to perceive and to be in awe and amazement as we look at eternity through spiritual eyes.

Earth's crammed with Heaven,
And every common bush afire with God;
But only he who sees, takes off his shoes,
The rest sit round it, and pluck blackberries.
Elizabeth Barrett Browning

Because Jesus is the Son of Man he knows what it is to be human. He knows what you are going through today. He understands your loss and grieving, loneliness and pain. He understands, for he has been on the path with you all of your days. You are not alone.

Because he is the Son of God, Jesus can forgive and heal, meeting us where we are and yet never leaving us the same. We have this moment to respond as did the paralytic on that day in Capernaum or we may choose to hold on to our scepticism as did the scholars. We can *see* or we can perceive with our spiritual eyes the truth of the Saviour who is in our presence.

Step out right now with extraordinary faith and cling to him. Really see.

Major Bente Gundersen
Rwanda and Burundi Command

God Does Things Differently
Luke 1:26-45

Introduction

GOD does things in surprising and unexpected ways. The verses about Mary and her cousin Elizabeth are for me an excellent example of the fact that God does things totally different from what we believe to be the best, totally different from what we imagine will bring the best result, and totally different from what we think is the best time.

The story of Mary and Elizabeth tells us about two women who were pregnant, but who were not really supposed to be or expected to be so. The way we meet these two women in the first chapter of Luke gives us a very good example of how God acts in surprising, different and unexpected ways. It shows us how God does not care if we think something is impossible, or whether we think something is fitting or normal or even a good idea.

For we have a God who is amazing and surprising – and more often than not he does things differently to what we expect or think he will do. God's thinking is not like our thinking, as Isaiah 55:8-9 says: "'For my thoughts are not your thoughts, neither are your ways my ways,' declares the Lord. "As the heavens are higher than the Earth, so are my ways higher than your ways and my thoughts than your thoughts.'"

As the apostle Paul puts it, God chooses differently to what we would choose. 'But God chose the foolish things of the world to shame the wise; God chose the weak things of the world to shame the strong. God chose the lowly things of this world and the despised things – and the things that are not – to nullify the things that are, so that no one may boast before him' (1 Corinthians 1:27-29).

Elizabeth and Mary

This whole story of Elizabeth and Mary is about two women – both expecting their first child. And neither of them was supposed to be pregnant, at least in the eyes of the society and the people around them.

Elizabeth

For Elizabeth it was because she was getting too old – and she had tried for too long. She was not able to have the child that her family, her husband and society expected from her. I'm sure that this had been a burden and a shame, casting a long dark shadow over her life. The fact of not being able to have a child was almost like an additional person in her marriage – the feeling of inadequacy and shame. The thought of not having a child was always there, following her wherever she went. And as she grew older she had even stopped hoping for a child; she had given up.

But God did not give up. An angel appeared to her husband Zechariah and told him that they would have a son. Zechariah doubted and said it was impossible – but Elizabeth became pregnant. Elizabeth knew. She recognised without a shadow of a doubt that God had made the impossible possible, and she knew this was God's doing. She knew that God does things surprisingly and differently from what we expect.

"'The Lord has done this for me," she said. "In these days he has shown his favour and taken away my disgrace among the people'" (Luke 1:25).

Elizabeth knew. God had done this – God had done this for her.

Mary

Mary, on the other hand, was not too old. She hadn't tried for too long either. On the contrary, the pregnancy would be a problem for her because she was too young and not yet married.

Research and tradition tell us that Mary was a young girl of about 14 years of age when the angel came to her. She was from Nazareth, a small and unimportant town. She was actually very much an ordinary young woman – and God chose to use her, an unmarried girl of 14 years, to bring Jesus our Saviour to the world. If we were there at the time and God had asked us what kind of woman he should use, would we have suggested a 14-year-old girl, not yet married? Maybe not – but God does things differently.

But as much as she was a normal girl in her community, at the same time she must have been a girl with a good strong relationship with God. And she was not easily scared or disturbed. The Bible tells of Old Testament prophets who, when they met with angels, were scared and awed in their presence. Mary was close to God. She knew the Scriptures well; and the word of God was a part of her. In Luke 1:46-49 we find the words that Mary used as her song of praise, referring back to Hannah's Prayer in 1 Samuel 2:1-10: 'My soul glorifies the Lord and my spirit rejoices in God my Saviour, for he has been mindful of the humble state of his servant. From now on all generations will call me blessed, for the Mighty One has done great things for me – holy is his name.'

But with Mary, something was different: the angel greeted her with respect. She was a young unmarried girl and for someone to meet her with great respect like this was unheard of in that culture. On the contrary, she was the one to greet first and show proper respect and politeness to almost everyone. She was of a low standing in her society – she was a young woman, just a girl, and she was unmarried. But here God's archangel shows respect to Mary. We may imagine that Mary was a bit worried because of this strange and unusual way of greeting her.

And we know: God does things differently and surprisingly.

When the angel greeted Mary he said, 'Greetings, you who are highly favoured! The Lord is with you' (v 28). When Mary was upset with this very respectful and unexpected greeting and wondered what was happening, the angel repeated the words and they became more than a greeting – it was a fact. 'Do not be afraid, Mary, you have found favour with God' (v 30). Some translations say it like this: 'You have been given grace'.

And what did Mary do? She was quite practical about it. She showed no fear; she didn't run away. She simply asked, 'How will this be…since

I am I virgin?' (v 34). And then she heard the angel's answer. I think Mary experienced her answer as a revelation from God, a confirmation and a certainty, and she was convinced. She was convinced, not because she understood but simply because she knew this was God. It was God who said and did this. This was his word to her and his will for her. Mary knew, as Elizabeth did, that this was God acting in her life. And she answered the angel, 'I am the Lord's servant...May your word to me be fulfilled' (v 38).

It was a revelation. It was not knowledge, it was not understanding, it was not credentials or qualifications. It was different, surprising and unexpected – but it was God. And Mary knew it was God talking to her, God who called her and wanted her to do what he told her, and she simply said: 'I am his servant'.

And she knew God had done this. God had done this for her.

God's grace and blessings

When Elizabeth saw Mary coming she ended her prophetic saying with these words, 'Blessed is she who has believed that the Lord would fulfil his promises to her!' (v 45). Elizabeth's prophetic saying as well as the angel's message describes Mary to us: 'You have found favour with God'. Mary had found favour with God and was blessed because she believed that what God said would happen! This is a starting point. It is a condition of life for Mary, and for us, because it brings back to us that the condition for God's favour and blessings is the answer Mary gave the angel: 'I am the Lord's servant, let it happen to me as you have said.'

God does things surprisingly, differently, unexpectedly – he uses people who are not big or important, he simply uses people who know him and love him and are willing to say as Mary: 'I am the Lord's servant, let it happen to me as you have said'.

For Elizabeth, God made the impossible possible. And Elizabeth is the one saying, 'Blessed are you who believed what the Lord has said' and consequently reminds us that the abundance of God's grace and blessings lies hidden in the response we give when God speaks to us.

Elizabeth knew God had done this – God had done this for her.

Mary was just a young girl, not highly respected or highly qualified. Her qualifications were simply her attitude and courage and her relationship with God. God had given her favour and grace and a confirmation that he was God in her life. And Mary responded, 'I am his servant'. She is eternally blessed because she believed that what God said would happen.

Mary knew God had done this – God had done this for her.

What about us?

God has already shown us his favour – we are saved by his grace. God does things surprisingly and differently. He has given us his favour, his grace and his blessings. And just as it was strange for Mary to be met with great respect from the angel – and not expected or deserved in the eyes of society – so are we undeserving in receiving God's grace and salvation.

But it doesn't stop with our salvation. God acts in unexpected ways in our lives, and he surprises us with his word and his revelations. He surprises us when we are in difficult situations and he gives us his peace and comfort. He surprises us by his calling and his words and sometimes even more when we feel his blessing when we respond to him. He surprises us when he reminds us in the middle of our daily chores that he loves us, and tells us again that we have his grace, his favour and his blessings.

He surprises us with new revelation from his word and from his Holy Spirit. He acts in unexpected ways when he gives us courage and revelation in our lives with him. He surprises us when we see that our motives and needs are transformed according to his will and his grace. And we know God has done this – God has done this for me.

God does not care who we are, but only cares how we respond to him. He has saved us and called us and he has something to say to us today and every day.

As Mary responded to the angel and to God, God asks us today if we are ready to say, 'I am the Lord's servant – let it happen to me as God has said'.

So may we live our lives and know that God has done this – God has done this for me.

Captain Jennifer Hale
Canada and Bermuda Territory

That's My King!
Matthew 21:1-11

JESUS' triumphal entry into Jerusalem, traditionally known as Palm Sunday, was the Sunday before Jesus was crucified, and the Passover Festival was about to begin. It's interesting to note that Jesus chose to announce he was the Messiah at a time when Jews from all of Israel would gather in Jerusalem to celebrate their exodus from Egypt. There would have been huge crowds and people who had either seen Jesus before or who heard of his ministry and would be excited to see him.

People seem to get excited over royalty, don't they? We seem to be fascinated with their lifestyle, their wealth and their relationships. People buy magazines and books to read the latest gossip on the royal family. I'm thinking in particular of Prince Charles and Princess Diana – people had a fascination with Princess Diana and the fascination continues with the prince's relationship with Camilla, Duchess of Cornwall.

But it's not just the royal family we are irresistibly drawn to. The world has made many 'kings'. I'm thinking of the king of rock 'n' roll – Elvis Presley. People were enthralled with Elvis because his performance style was enormously popular and controversial. Elvis's home, Graceland, was opened as a museum in 1982 and it receives more than 600,000 visitors annually. It is the second most visited home in the United States of America after the White House.

Then there's the king of pop – Michael Jackson. He was recognised as the most successful and influential entertainer of all time. He became a global figure in popular culture for more than 40 years and Jackson's contributions to the music industry led to his personal life being publicised.

When you think of Egyptian royalty, who comes to mind? King Tutankhamun, of course! The 1922 discovery of King Tutankhamun's intact tomb received worldwide press coverage and sparked a renewed interest in ancient Egypt.

It seems the world has many kings. However, we do not continually celebrate the birth of an earthly king, for earthly kings come and go, their popularity fades over time and their kingdom is only temporary. Rather, we celebrate the King of all kings, the Lord of all lords, Jesus Christ.

In Zechariah 9:9 *NIV 1984* you will see the events of Palm Sunday prophesied more than 500 years before they happened. The verse says: 'Rejoice greatly, O Daughter of Zion! Shout, Daughter of Jerusalem! See, your king comes to you, righteous and having salvation, gentle and riding on a donkey, on a colt, the foal of a donkey.' This is one of the most specific messianic prophecies in the Old Testament and it was fulfilled when Jesus made his triumphal entry into Jerusalem as a sign to them that he was their Messiah.

However, the people who were praising God for giving them a king on this day had the wrong idea about Jesus. They were expecting a political king who would overthrow the Roman government. They were so focused on their desire for a new national leader that their ears were deaf to the words of the prophets in the Old Testament. When it became obvious that Jesus was not the king they were looking for, many turned their backs on him and, perhaps, were in the crowd later that week shouting 'Crucify him!'.

The wave of public opinion does not change who Jesus was then and who he is now. Jesus is the king and that is what Palm Sunday is all about, a confirmation and public proclamation of Jesus' kingship. So, when we prepare to celebrate Easter, let us allow Scripture to affirm for us what it did for the crowds 2,000 years ago – that Jesus is our king!

Jesus' kingship goes well beyond Palm Sunday, and as we affirm him as our king let us remember first of all that Jesus was born a king!

In the narrative of Jesus' birth, the Magi came from the east to

Jerusalem and asked: 'Where is he that is born King of the Jews?' (Matthew 2:2 *KJV*). The visit and worship of the wise men was recorded to authenticate the kingship of Jesus. These men from faraway lands recognised Jesus as the Messiah when most of God's chosen people in Israel did not.

In Luke 1:31-33 *NIV 1984* the angel says to Mary, 'You will be with child and give birth to a son, and you are to give him the name Jesus. He will be great and will be called the Son of the Most High. The Lord God will give him the throne of his father David, and he will reign over the house of Jacob forever; his kingdom will never end.' Centuries earlier, God had promised David that his kingdom would last forever, and we see fulfilment of the prophecy in 2 Samuel 7:16. This promise was fulfilled in the coming of Jesus, a direct descendant of David, whose reign will continue throughout eternity.

The prophet Isaiah proclaimed his kingship; 'For to us a child is born, to us a son is given, and the government will be on his shoulders. And he will be called Wonderful Counsellor, Mighty God, Everlasting Father, Prince of Peace. Of the increase of his government and peace there will be no end. He will reign on David's throne and over his kingdom, establishing and upholding it with justice and righteousness from that time on and forever. The zeal of the Lord Almighty will accomplish this' (Isaiah 9:6-7 *NIV 1984*).

In a time of great darkness, God promised to send a light that would shine on everyone living in the shadow of death. This message of hope was fulfilled in the birth of Christ and the establishment of his eternal Kingdom. He came to deliver all people from their slavery to sin. Jesus was not made a king, he was born a king. He has always been king and always will be king. His birth narrative reminds us that his kingship is eternal. John 1:1 tells us, 'In the beginning was the Word…' Jesus was king of creation before time even began, he was king when he came to Earth as a helpless baby, and he will still be king when he comes back for his bride at the end of time!

Jesus needs no credentials or testimony from man to affirm who he is. There isn't anything you and I can do, there was nothing Pilate, the Jewish leaders or Herod could have done, and there is nothing the world can say or do to alter that. Jesus was born a king! Not only was he born a king but we see proof of his kingship throughout his earthly ministry and in particular his triumphal entry into Jerusalem.

We can see that Jesus had the power of a king! The Bible tells us in Luke 19:39-40 that '…the Pharisees in the crowd said to Jesus, "Teacher, rebuke your disciples!" "I tell you," he replied, "if they keep quiet, the stones will cry out."' Can you imagine what the Pharisees might have thought about those statements? No doubt they thought they were blasphemous and they certainly didn't want their authority challenged. So they asked Jesus to keep his people quiet. But Jesus said that if the people were quiet, the stones would immediately cry out. Why? Not because Jesus was setting up a powerful political kingdom, but because he was establishing God's eternal Kingdom.

We also find verses such as Psalm 96:11 *KJV* that say, 'Let the heavens rejoice, and let the Earth be glad; let the sea roar, and the fullness thereof.' And the majestic verse 12 in Isaiah chapter 55 that speaks of the mountains and the hills breaking forth into song and the trees of the fields clapping their hands. Or Habakkuk 2:11, which has a direct relation to our text when it says 'the stones of the wall will cry out', and in Job 38:7 where there is reference to the morning stars singing together. These verses suggest that creation acknowledges the power and authority of God.

We can also think of Jesus' power over the wind and the waves when he calmed the storm. Even when Christ was crucified, we read of the sun refusing to shine, the Earth shaking and the rocks splitting apart. So Jesus was not confused when he said that if his disciples were silent the stones would cry out!

Jesus was born a king, Jesus has the power of a king and finally we see that Jesus has the heart of a king!

One of the qualities of a good leader is compassion. Jesus was compassionate; he had a heart for people. In the Palm Sunday narrative in Luke chapter 19, as Jesus approached Jerusalem and saw the city, he was weeping. Verses 41-44 say: 'As he approached Jerusalem and saw the city, he wept over it and said, "If you, even you, had only known on this day what would bring you peace – but now it is hidden from your eyes. The days will come upon you when your enemies will build an embankment against you and encircle you and hem you in on every side. They will dash you to the ground, you and the children within your walls. They will not leave one stone on another, because you did not recognise the time of God's coming to you.'"

The Prince of Peace was in town. Human hands could touch the Redeemer, the Saviour of the world – and they missed him! Not unlike us sometimes, they wanted God on their terms. They were waiting for a warrior, a ruler and a king with an earthly throne and crown and instead they received a saviour, a servant – a man hanging on a cross. They didn't understand that Jesus had come to free their souls and not their cities. In this text we see a picture of Jesus weeping over Jerusalem saying, 'If you only knew! You are headed for destruction but I have come to save you.'

I believe Jesus weeps over our world today. In our western world we have churches on every street corner but we are missing God's presence in our midst. Jesus looks out over our cities today and sees troubled parents. He sees people with drug and alcohol addiction, he sees women having abortions and suffering sexual abuse. He looks out and sees the graves of teenagers, who died prematurely at the hands of their own classmates, gunned down at school. He sees lives that are torn apart, kids without families, hearts that are empty, suicide, rape, murder, incest, divorce, hatred and pornography. He sees it and he weeps.

I also want to suggest to you that Jesus not only weeps for our cities but he weeps for you. He knows you intimately and weeps over the brokenness in your life. Jesus, who is now at the right hand of our heavenly Father, wants to be king in your life. He wants to right the wrongs in life. What Satan means for evil, Jesus wants to use for good. And so I say to you – that's my King! Is he yours?

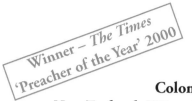

Colonel Margaret Hay
New Zealand, Fiji and Tonga Territory

The People Who Walked in Darkness Have Seen a Great Light

Isaiah 9:2-7

I KNOCKED at the cell door and squinted through the hatch into the darkness. Then eyes met mine; a light went on. 'I'm Margaret, from chaplaincy. Can I come in?' 'Yeah, Miss, come. What time is it, Miss? What day is it?' Another young man hibernating in hell, sleeping away his sorrow in the sump.

Once more I heard of sins and scars, and then I left; the bolt banged, and I looked back through the hatch to see him leaning against the top bunk crying. And the word of the Lord came from Isaiah 9:2 *NRSV*:

The people who walked in darkness
have seen a great light;
those who lived in a land of deep darkness, on them light has shined.

Just as sounds reverberate in prison wings, so the prophet's words resonated in my head. Words rooted in historical events – the devastation of the northern land of Israel about 733 BC – but written with bold confidence, past and future tenses alternating, subtly anticipating a unified land under an ideal future ruler. The ancient text, grounded in the history of Israel and Jewish prophecy, resounded across the ages to that cell in Brixton:

Those who lived in a land of deep darkness – on them light has shined.

The word was a kindled flame, a sign of God's hope for that weeping man, and for the entire human community.

Believing so, Christians, with boldness and yet with awe, follow our Lord in describing his ministry in the light of texts from Isaiah – as Luther put it: 'Reading the Bible forwards but understanding it backwards.'

My work is with remand and convicted prisoners, and also with asylum seekers being held, sometimes for many months, in prison conditions – people with dreams, experiences, anxieties and great questions. Outside prison it might be hard to talk about these things, but inside it's normal. And the Word speaks with power to us seekers and sinners, the intensity of the divine presence being unmistakable as the Spirit intercedes for God's beloved, bent world.

Again this Advent, prisoners and asylum seekers from some of the world's most dangerous destinations will hear Isaiah's words (v 4):

For the yoke of their burden,
and the bar across their shoulders,
the rod of their oppressor,
you have broken as on the day of Midian.

The three images of oppression – yoke, staff [bar] and rod – are destroyed as in the victory of Gideon over the Midianites. Reading this, I remember a South African re-enacting such deliverance, uncoiling himself from a foetal crouch and suddenly lifting his head and flinging his shoulders back as he quietly said, 'I was oppressed'.

Underlying the prophet Isaiah's words you can hear the rhythm of oppression: pomp and ceremony, power and secrecy. But if you have ears you can hear a different drum somewhere in the distance. Instead of 'the yoke of their burden' there is another – 'My yoke is easy and my burden

86

is light'. Instead of 'the boots of the tramping warriors' we have 'the beautiful feet of the messenger who announces peace'. In fact, the whole military paraphernalia is now surplus to requirements (v 5):

For all the boots of the tramping warriors
and all the garments rolled in blood
shall be burned as fuel for the fire.

It's the sound of a different drum, all right. The people who walked in darkness are on a very different sort of march: steady, persistent, joyful. You can hear songs of freedom and shouts of delight. It's a ramshackle outfit, it's true, outrageously inclusive, a mighty moving crowd from the east and the west, many coming out of great tribulation, some weeping, some dancing, some being carried, all exulting and rejoicing. Why the excitement? Because of what Isaiah said (v 6):

For a child has been born for us,
a son given to us;

Words originally with a particular local meaning, but reverberating for Christians in the light of God in Christ. For our sakes a child was born; as the Book of Wisdom 18:14-15 describes it:

While all things were in quiet silence,
And the night was in the midst of her course,
Your almighty Word leapt down from Heaven,
From your royal throne, as a fierce conqueror,
Into the midst of the land of destruction.

The Christ child, 'pink and white with cheeks so rosy' as we used to sing at school, is also the wild warrior battling for his beloved world. And there are victories to be seen – daily they're there.

I think of a man last week, at the end of his sentence, a refined man, restrained in the expression of his faith, telling of a mystical experience just

87

days before his release which he said could only be described by the word 'deliverance'.

I think of a mentally ill man asking in terror, 'Do you think that the Holy Spirit is after me?' I said that the Spirit is holding us securely and tenderly and surrounding us like the sun – mercifully that day it was shining after weeks of rain. And as we spoke a momentary look of comfort – and was it hope? – came into his eye.

And, again, I hold in my heart a picture of an asylum seeker coming in for worship a couple of Sundays ago, and going down on his knees, head in his hands, in thanksgiving for news of his imminent release after a long, anxious detention.

But not every battle against the darkness ends in victory. Sometimes the anxieties are too great and the light too much to bear – a reminder of Viktor Frankl's image of his fellow prisoners in Dachau: some, when freed, walked into the sunlight, blinked, then walked back into the familiar darkness. But still God is even there, and our darkness is no darkness to him.

The prophet Isaiah wrote a series of names, so well known from Handel's Messiah that it's hard just to say them – they have to be sung: 'Wonderful Counsellor, Mighty God, Everlasting Father, the Prince of Peace' – originally the throne names for an ideal king, but echoing through the universe as we behold our God.

Raymond Fung, in his book *Households of God on China's Soil*, writes of a Chinese man telling of his experiences in the Cultural Revolution, of his 'long march' to the countryside, and of how he became a Christian during that time. Reflecting on those testing years he said, 'I, at least, have my fellow Christians to turn to, a place where I pray and sing and let God's words flow over me. But it is not just for me. There are these millions of my generation. When I think of myself I think of them. When can we have another 'long march', hard and poor, but going together, sharing things together, not just serving people's dollars? Do you know if there is really such a thing as a Christian marching song?'

Yes, there is! Charles Wesley wrote it. It's this:

Hail the Heaven-born Prince of Peace!
Hail the Sun of righteousness!
Light and life to all he brings,
Risen with healing in his wings.
Mild he lays his glory by,
Born that man no more may die,
Born to raise the sons of earth,
Born to give them second birth.
SASB, No 82 v 3

And I want to run from cell to cell calling through the hatches, 'Wake up! Rise from the dead! And Christ will shine on you.'

'Christ!'

'Yes, Christ, Immanuel; it means "God with us". It's Advent; that means "coming". He's coming. He's come. God is with us; here in this prison. He said so. He is the "Wonderful Counsellor, Mighty God, Everlasting Father, Prince of Peace".'

Tonight those words will ring again around the dome of St Paul's Cathedral, and, this Advent, in buildings great and small, up and down the land and throughout the world. It's the news of the hour, as the ageing Zechariah understood in Luke 1:76-79 when he held his child, the baby John, the forerunner, in his arms, and said:

And you, child, will be called the prophet of the Most High;
for you will go before the Lord to prepare his ways,
to give knowledge of salvation to his people by the forgiveness of their sins.
By the tender mercy of our God,
the dawn from on high will break upon us,
to give light to those who sit in darkness and in the shadow of death,
to guide our feet into the way of peace.

Major Suzanne Hay
New Zealand, Fiji and Tonga Territory

Get the Rewards You Really Deserve

Genesis chapter 15

THE words 'Because Mum Deserves It' were splashed in bright pink across the top of the advertising mailshot I pulled out of my letter box. Apparently we mums deserve jewellery, clothing, perfume, linen, handbags, new TVs and chocolate! The advertisement failed to tell me why mums deserve any or all of the suggested gifts. However, given that Mother's Day was just around the corner, it seemed that being a mum was enough. According to the retailer's promotional material I deserved to be rewarded just for being a mum!

Some years ago a television advertising campaign in New Zealand encouraged all of us to 'Get the rewards you really deserve'. I recall these claims being supported by at least two television commercials: one had two men exhausting themselves as they cleaned up an older woman's very overgrown garden. Knocking on her door at the end of the day anticipating a cold drink and a fat cheque, they were baffled when the reward for their hard work was one small hen's egg each as payment!

In the second storyline a young girl painfully wrenched a tooth from her mouth with string tied to a brick in anticipation of a visit from the tooth fairy. Her disappointment was clear when all she found under her pillow was a miserly five-cent piece.

These advertising campaigns pick up on the facet of human nature that carries a sense of entitlement. Even the most noble of us have days when we expect recognition, when we feel we deserve to be rewarded for our efforts, or that we deserve better! Given that characters from the Bible often exhibit these very human qualities, it's not surprising to find that God spent time conversing with Abram about the rewards he expected.

Let's recap Abram's story up until the moment of this conversation: Abram, who later became known as Abraham, had been minding his own business, living with his family in Ur. We are told in Joshua 24:2 that Abram's father worshipped idols, so it's likely Abram followed the custom of his time and culture and also worshipped those idols.

Yet God found a way to get Abram's attention and offered him the chance to begin a relationship with a God he hardly knew. Did he deserve this reward? Not at all! He had done nothing to earn God's interest, love or recognition. The offer of a rewarding relationship with God came to Abram as an undeserved gift.

But wait, there's more! The gift offered to Abram came with a bonus offer – an invitation to embark on the process of becoming whole. He was promised the reward of wholeness. Abram's life was incomplete. He carried the bitter pain of being childless. In that day and culture, childlessness defined his identity. Without a child he had no heir and no future, no hope of comfort in his old age and no chance of his lineage being traced forwards as well as backwards. I suggest this pain created within him a vacuum that needed to be filled.

A significant step towards finding wholeness for Abram had to include him resolving this inner emptiness. God's very first encounter with him was a promise that did just that –God's offer of relationship included the promise that he would become the patriarch of a great nation. And so God met Abram at his point of greatest need. God offered to address his lack of wholeness.

The invitation to become whole required something of Abram, however. Abram must leave his old life – the familiar people, places and possessions that defined his past. The promise to become whole could only be fulfilled as Abram partnered with God on a journey of faith, trust, and a new approach to life.

Abram accepted God's invitation. With little to go on, Abram started to move away from his father's influence, and began to worship this new God. Abram literally took a step of faith and left his old way of being, taking with him his childless wife and reckless nephew, along with animals and employees to support his new life. Together they embarked on a long journey towards a new land of promise.

In the process Abram and his nephew, Lot, enlarged their fortunes and needed to separate so they wouldn't compete with each other for food, water and grazing. About this time war broke out and Lot became a prisoner of war. Abram mounted a rescue effort and was so successful he impressed some local kings who wanted to acknowledge and reward his abilities. Abram, however, turned down the rewards they offered, telling them he would trust God to reward him with everything he needed. He really was beginning to grow in his relationship with God. It is at this point that we pick up the story.

I'm imagining Abram walked away from the battle and the dialogue with the kings (described in Genesis chapter 14) with mixed emotions. He would have felt the jubilation of victory, relief at securing Lot's safe return, and pride at the response of the kings to his prowess and skill. Yet I suggest part of him was also terrified: he may have impressed five kings with his victory, but he had severely annoyed another four by defeating them! He must have been worried that those four angry kings would seek their revenge.

In the middle of this emotional mix the Bible reports: 'After this, the word of the Lord came to Abram in a vision' (Genesis 15:1). Translators do not really know what the author meant by the word 'vision'. Certainly 'vision' is not such a surprising description of what happened here, given that Abram was experiencing a heightened state of emotional intensity. Let's unpack this encounter with God to learn truths to help our own spiritual journey towards the reward of wholeness.

The conversation begins; 'Do not be afraid, Abram.' Once again God engages with Abram at his point of greatest need; assuming Abram was terrified of his new enemies, God's first words, 'Do not be afraid' were exactly the reassurance he needed. In the face of fear God says, 'Do not be afraid, Abram'. God had the situation in hand. God was in control.

I wonder if Abram was able to grasp hold of God's reassurance in that moment. When he heard the words, 'Do not be afraid', I wonder if he smiled politely, whilst inwardly thinking 'I don't think so!'. I wonder if he was so afraid that he was unable to trust God. I wonder if he was really thinking, 'God is not the answer to this problem'. I wonder if he had decided God would not be enough for him in this moment of crisis.

God seemed to anticipate such doubt by adding further words of reassurance: 'Do not be afraid, Abram. I am your shield'. The image of a shield conveyed to Abram an image of God protecting him. The creator of the universe was declaring he would defend Abram. God would come between Abram and his enemies. God would protect him. He promised Abram that God alone was all he needed in that moment.

God continued the conversation: 'I am...your very great reward'. Abram had just turned down great wealth following his battle victory. God recognised this act with the promise of an even better reward – God. God himself was to be his reward. God would fulfil and complete him. God would be everything to him.

'I am your very great reward,' says God. This was potentially a deeply moving moment. Yet Abram stamped his foot and retorted in verse two, 'What can you give me...I remain childless'. Abram essentially said to God, 'It's not you I want. Give me the reward I really deserve.' His very human response conveyed the deep ache that remained within his heart and defined his life – he was childless and without an heir or a future.

God didn't recoil in the face of his honest and human reactions. God didn't throw a lightning bolt or demand a confession of self-centredness. God understood Abram was just starting his journey to wholeness, and needed some help on this day. God graciously and patiently reminded Abram of the original promise – he *would* have a son. And just for a moment Abram believed it – but only for a moment. It wasn't long before he turned around to God and demanded, 'Prove it'.

And God did just that. God granted Abram a tangible sign of a promise that he could only sense by faith at that time. At God's command Abram prepared animals for sacrifice and at nightfall God sent a flame.

94

God gave Abram proof in a way that made sense in his culture and context. The contract was sealed.

Abram was 99 years old when his wife conceived. For those of us who seek quick fixes or desire instant gratification that is not very reassuring! God's gift to Abram was not an 'Instant Kiwi' [lottery prize] kind of reward, but a growing investment, a reward that grew as Abram strengthened his relationship with this loving divine authority. It was a reward that grew as he continued to talk to God about his deepest pain – childlessness – and the fear that this would never be resolved.

Hear God's words to Abram; 'Do not be afraid, Abram. I am your shield, your very great reward.' Hear God's words to us; 'Do not be afraid. I am your shield. I am your very great reward.'

I am reminded of God's somewhat cryptic words to Moses: 'I am who I am' (Exodus 3:14). The phrase can also be rendered 'I will be what I will be'. The title portrays the idea that God is enough for all we experience and go through, that God will be all we need. The words were later used up by Jesus in a series of 'I am' claims to suggest he is also all we need or, to put it another way, Jesus is totally sufficient – the all-encompassing solution for everything we experience.

Ultimately the invitation of God to Abram was to trust him with every part of his life, including the most vulnerable depths of his inner being. The outcome of embracing this invitation was a journey towards wholeness, and the discovery that God alone would soothe and satisfy the innermost longings of his soul.

The truth of the Abram story is that God *became* all Abram needed him to be over the course of their journey together. As the story unfolds Abram trusted then doubted, trusted then doubted, time and time again. Over time the periods of trust started to dominate. God did address the anguish of his soul. God did become his very great reward. Not 'the reward he really deserved', for he was as flawed and human as the rest of us, but God understood his doubt, God understood he was very human, and partnered Abram on a journey towards wholeness.

As with Abram, our relationship with God is as a gift. It is the gift of personal connection with the Creator of the universe. Our gift-wrapped package is always undeserved, never earned. Offered, never forced. An invitation, never a demand. This allows us the freedom to accept (or decline) it and then unwrap God's gift at our own pace.

Like Abram we will discover God's gift of relationship comes with a bonus offer to embark on a costly journey towards wholeness. Such a journey involves us leaving behind previous ways of being, as we trust ourselves to the care of God; even the parts of ourselves that are most vulnerable – the character flaws we struggle to accept, the pain we cannot face, the things we fear God cannot fix, the behaviours we are too ashamed to speak about, the fear that we are not enough, the circumstances we decide we do not deserve because they are too hard, or the experiences we believe we do not deserve because they are too good and we are too unworthy.

The journey towards wholeness is about learning to trust God with all of this. It is normal to face such a journey of trust with some anxiety. God reassures us: 'Do not be afraid'.

Let's be honest. Like Abram we can fail to grasp God's reassurance, or like Abram we grasp it for a time, but then a new challenge confronts us and we struggle again. Abram reminds us that this is a very normal part of the process of becoming whole. Even when we, like Abram, protest and cry out to God, 'You aren't enough, you haven't fixed me yet, I want the reward now', the gift is still extended to us. In the face of such responses God continues to give far more than we really deserve. God works with our doubts rather than dismissing them. God graciously accepts our tantrums, our attempts to fix our own lives, and our demands to receive the reward of wholeness without experiencing the process of becoming whole. God understands we will need help with the process and he whispers, 'Do not be afraid'.

As we participate in the journey towards wholeness, God's intention is to address the areas of our lives where we are incomplete. God knows our points of greatest need and offers 'I am' promises to perfectly match our personal disposition.

In the face of our inner hunger Jesus promises 'I am The Bread of Life'; when we struggle with uncertainty Jesus reminds us 'I am The Way'; when we feel trapped Jesus claims, 'I am The Gate'; when our world is in darkness he declares, 'I am The Light'. Whatever our situation or need Jesus is clear – 'I am enough'. Even when we protest and doubt, even when we insist on proof, even when we demand the rewards we think we really deserve, God keeps on patiently promising to complete us. God *is* all we need. God will be all we need. God will be our very great reward.

In conclusion, the gift of relationship is free but the process which follows is costly. The gift needs our acceptance and the process requires courage. The promise is that we will become whole, for the reward is God, who completes us. Not the reward we really deserve, but the reward we receive as we risk trusting our lives to God.

May God grant us each the courage to embrace his promise: 'Do not be afraid. I am your shield. I am your very great reward.'

Major Heather Jenkins
Australia Southern Territory

Faith Under Fire

Daniel 3:19-20

Introduction

THERE are times in life when we feel as if we are in the furnace and someone has their hand on the thermostat.

This is how my husband and I felt when he faced some serious health issues. We thought we took the news fairly calmly. We had been through similar times of stress with others and now here we were 'in the furnace'. I shed some tears, but tried to remain positive as my husband went through the tests. We mobilised an army of prayers. A week later, we faced news of the worst scenario. The furnace was hot and getting hotter.

How do you cope with that? How do you cope with heat of any kind? Ill health, relationship trauma, financial worries, the doubt of faith? How do you cope? What do you do?

Daniel chapter three tells the story of three godly Jewish men who were quite literally thrown into the fire!

Shadrach, Meshach and Abednego, along with Daniel, had been brought from Judah into exile in Babylon. They were assigned to the palace of King Nebuchadnezzar where they were trained in the ways of the Babylonians. The king was so impressed with them that he appointed them to become advisers in the royal court and eventually they were put in charge of the affairs of the province of Babylon (Daniel 2:49).

King Nebuchadnezzar had a huge gold statue built and commanded everyone to bow down and worship. Anyone who refused would be thrown into the furnace. Shadrach, Meshach and Abednego bravely refused! They refused to bow down to an idol. They refused to be brought down in fear. They refused to hide their love for their God. And so they were thrown into the fire – a fire so intense that even the guards died.

What had gone wrong? One moment they were safe, the next they were tossed into what seemed to be certain death.

These men had faithfully obeyed God, and now this! A hotter-than-hot furnace! But the furnace, the fire, which should have ended their lives, turned out to be the place where they met God. God delivered Shadrach, Meshach and Abednego in the furnace, not from it. And he will do the same for us!

Fires will come!

The Bible does not guarantee us freedom from the fires and storms of life. In fact, the Bible is filled with references to the fact that storms will come. They will be part and parcel of the life of every believer. And the experience of my husband and me confirms that!

Fires will come, but Scripture says that God will be with us in the furnace! When King Nebuchadnezzar looked into the furnace he saw not just Shadrach, Meshach and Abednego in the flames, he saw a fourth man there! 'He said, "Look! I see four men walking around in the fire, unbound and unharmed, and the fourth looks like a son of the gods"' (Daniel 3:25).

We don't like the fire. We don't like painful circumstances. If we could we would find a way of escape. But some of our most intense periods of spiritual growth come in the flames. In the flames we discover the presence of God. We learn the truth of Scripture's promises, such as: 'I will never leave you nor forsake you' (Joshua 1:5).

'Do not be fainthearted or afraid; do not panic or be terrified by them. For the Lord your God is the one who goes with you to fight for you against your enemies to give you victory' (Deuteronomy 20:3-4).

Such truths come alive for us in the heat of the fire. Like a dormant seed opens up when fires sweep through the forest. Fires will come, but God will meet us in the furnace.

Offer the fire to the Lord!

Shadrach, Meshach and Abednego knew their limitations. They knew that they were unable to face the furnace alone. They offered the 'fire' of their circumstance to the Lord. They said, 'If we are thrown into the blazing furnace, the God we serve is able to deliver us from it, and he will deliver us from your majesty's hand' (Daniel 3:17).

In the first chapter of Daniel, when these men had first arrived in Babylon, they took their stand for God and committed themselves to live for him and for him alone. They resisted the temptation to blend in, to compromise, to deny their faith. In the third chapter they are faced with death and yet they are determined to serve the Lord. Their faith, shaped in earlier days, stood in the day of extreme testing!

And they said more: 'If we are thrown into the blazing furnace, the God we serve is able to deliver us from it, and he will deliver us from your majesty's hand. But even if he does not, we want you to know, your majesty, that we will not serve your gods or worship the image of gold you have set up' (Daniel 3:17-18).

These are the words of great faith! Yes, the fire was uncomfortable. Yes, it was hot. Yes, the fire could destroy them. However, as they faced the fire they were given grace to 'faith' the fire! They knew that, even if they were thrown into the fire, even if God did not rescue them from the flames, they would still trust in God. That is an amazing victory! Not just a victory over flames, but victory over fear, the victory of trust in God.

At times we will find ourselves in difficult places. We pray for grace to know the presence of God in that place. And he graciously assures us that he is with us. And sometimes rescue comes! Dramatically! Miraculously! But it is no less a miracle when God's people endure the fire with little relief, and still say with faith, 'Even if he does not, we will not serve your god'. This is the miracle of victory over fear, the miracle of trust in the eternal God who holds us in his hands through eternity.

Faith the fire!

So when fires come, offer your fire to the Lord and 'faith the fire'! Know that you will never face the flames alone. Know that God will meet you in the blaze and he will strengthen you in your present difficulties. Know that the God we serve is all-powerful and is able to take care of his children now and through eternity.

Know that in the fire our faith can be purified and refined, deepened and strengthened as we cast ourselves on God. Know that faith, refined by fire, glorifies God to those around us.

When Nebuchadnezzar ordered Shadrach, Meshach and Abednego to come out of the furnace, he praised their God and noted their courage, saying, 'Praise be to the God of Shadrach, Meshach and Abednego, who has sent his angel and rescued his servants! They trusted in him and defied the king's command and were willing to give up their lives rather than serve or worship any god except their own God' (Daniel 3:28).

Reflection

What is the 'fire' you face? Picture God present with you in that furnace. Hear him say to you, 'Do not fear, for I have redeemed you; I have summoned you by name; you are mine. When you pass through the waters, I will be with you; and when you pass through the rivers, they will not sweep over you. When you walk through the fire, you will not be burned; the flames will not set you ablaze. For I am the Lord, your God, the Holy One of Israel, your Saviour...' (Isaiah 43:1-3).

'Faith the fire' and trust him to lead you through.

Major Tracey Kasuso
Southern Africa Territory

Trust in God
Proverbs 3:5-6

Introduction

THE story is told of a little girl and her father who were walking across a bridge. The father, concerned for his daughter's safety, said to her: 'Sweetheart, please hold my hand so that you do not fall into the river.' The little girl replied: 'No, Dad, you hold my hand! If I hold your hand and something happens to me, the chances are that I may let go of you, but if you hold me I know with certainty that no matter what happens you will never let me fall.'

Trust is an integral part of all relationships and the bond of love. So hold on to the hand of God who you trust and who loves and cares for you. God is looking for followers who will trust him with their lives.

I would like us to look at these verses: 'Trust in the Lord with all your heart and lean not on your own understanding; in all your ways acknowledge him, and he will make your paths straight' (Proverbs 3:5-6 *NIV 1984*).

'Trust in the Lord with all your heart'

What does that mean to 'trust in the Lord with all your heart?' In Proverbs 4:23 *NIV 1984* we read: 'Above all else, guard your heart, for it is the wellspring of life'. In a nutshell this is the answer to trusting the Lord wholeheartedly. We are to guard our hearts by fighting off doubt from entering and polluting the river of our lives. It's about trusting God with all that is in us. It means giving all of the strength we possess, both physical and mentally, to do the will of God.

103

Simply believing in God is a good starting point for us, but we also need to have faith and trust, which is the practical outworking of faith. On a daily basis we have to trust so many people; when we are sick we trust the doctors to heal us, builders to build our house so that it is not going to fall in on our heads, and pilots to fly us safely to our destinations.

The word 'all' indicates that we are to trust God with the 'whole' of our lives. Trusting God requires total commitment. There is no room for a 'pick-and-mix' trust in God for our children and our relationships. Let us not be content with where we are today but have a desire to grow spiritually. God is challenging us to enter into a deeper relationship with him, so allow him to show you that you can trust him with every aspect of your life. Believe in the omnipotent and omniscient God whose decisions are perfect.

'Lean not on your own understanding'

If God is central in our lives we can deduce that we live for him alone. There are two paths here for us to explore: one is leaning on our own understanding, the other is leaning on God's understanding. Our way is limited but God's way is unlimited.

When we get into difficult and complex situations in life and we cannot see our way, or when we feel like we're heading for a storm, we need to 'lean' on God for guidance because we do not want to be crushed by the storms of life. We may feel that our lives are moving swimmingly and that we are heading in the right direction, but the only certainty we have is knowing that we're at the centre of God's will for our lives by placing our trust in his word and works.

Solomon is a good example of this. He began his reign as King of Israel brilliantly. He asked God for wisdom then built a magnificent temple so that people could worship the one true God. This pleased God, and Solomon grew in wisdom and stature, and became famous for this, but then sadly went his own way.

The Bible tells us that Solomon acquired an army for himself, imported horses from Egypt, accumulated vast amounts of silver and gold, and built himself a palace more beautiful than the one he constructed for

God. He had 700 wives and 300 concubines, his power went to his head and he began to oppress the people. This resulted in splitting the kingdom and led to the eventual destruction of the nation.

A word of caution: this can happen in our own lives. If we 'lean' on our own strength rather than placing our faith and trust in God, our lives could also end in ruin. We need God's constant guiding hand and wisdom in our lives.

'In all your ways acknowledge him'

This is a call to acknowledge God in every part of our lives. We often sing this stirring song of consecration:

All to Jesus I surrender,
All to him I freely give;
I will ever love and trust him,
In his presence daily live.
SASB, No 474 v 1

It is my prayer, that we not only sing these words, but also that we are inspired to live them. There is no point in saying that God is everything on a Sunday morning, and then on Monday in the office closing the door on him! It is important to acknowledge God in all our ways. We all have parts of our lives which we keep separate from God. It could be our finances, our employment, our marriage or our lifestyle. In a way we are saying to God 'I can manage this on my own'. Even if you are absolutely sure you are in God's will, we need to surrender to God, saying; 'Not my will Lord, but yours'.

'And he will make your paths straight'

Here is the blessing, a promise and the joy of it all: 'He will make your paths straight'. In other words God is saying trust me, do it my way and I will show you that I am able. He is able to make our crooked paths straight. Remember, Jesus came to give us life – in all its fullness.

God's path is not one that our sinful natures automatically follow. At times there seem to be insurmountable obstacles before us, which cause us to doubt that this is the 'straight path' that God is leading us on. Don't despair – this is all part of the learning process of trusting in the Lord with all our hearts. Removing the obstructions is his job! 'He will make your paths straight.' In Jeremiah 29:11 we read: '"For I know the plans I have for you," declares the Lord, "plans to prosper you and not to harm you, plans to give you hope and a future"'.

Trust in the Lord and allow him to direct you. Be encouraged and continue to put your trust in our heavenly Father.

Major Paula Knight
Brazil Territory

Are You a Roof-breaker?

Mark 2:1-12

Introduction

I THINK that God has a sense of humour because at a time when we are having the leaky roof of our hall repaired he has led me to share a story of four men who broke a roof. I hope it will be an inspiration for us as we think about the conviction, courage and compassion of these men who were so convinced that Jesus could heal their friend they were prepared to put their reputation on the line and do everything they possibly could do to make sure that Jesus saw him. A typical house in Palestine was like a square box with a staircase on the outside going up to the roof. The roof was made of separate tiles that could be lifted up and replaced. When the men arrived at the house where Jesus was teaching, and found a large crowd both inside and outside, they carried their paralysed friend up the outside staircase and lifted the roof tiles to lower him down to Jesus. It was quite an achievement and would have taken a great deal of effort.

Convinced

What would make a group of friends act like this? To be so determined that they would carry their friend to the house where Jesus was teaching and persevere even when the crowd was so large they couldn't enter the house? How could they be so bold as to carry their friend up to the roof, take up the tiles and lower him into the room below? Why would anyone act like this? They must have been absolutely convinced that Jesus had the power to heal their friend.

Jesus said, 'I am the way and the truth and the life. No one comes to the Father except through me' (John 14:6). I don't know if these men understood theology but we can see by their actions that they believed they had found the truth. If they didn't really believe in Jesus they would not have made such an effort.

It took four of them to carry their friend. Have you ever tried to carry another person with three other people? Each person must walk in the same direction and at the same pace; otherwise, the person being carried will be dropped. It is not an easy task. You would only do something like that if you were convinced that it would be worthwhile. They had obviously heard about Jesus and maybe even met him before or seen him heal other people. The Bible does not tell us these details; however, we can see from their actions that they were willing to put their trust in Jesus.

When I was a student I heard an evangelist say that the reason some Christians do not share their faith is because they are not really convinced that Jesus is the only way. Nor do they really believe that if one does not put their trust in Jesus that they will not go to Heaven when they die. The Bible contains the words of Jesus as remembered and recorded by the people who met him and knew him.

Jesus said, 'I am the way and the truth and the life. No one comes to the Father except through me' (John 14:6). When he said those words to his disciples Philip replied, 'Lord, show us the Father and that will be enough for us' (John 14:8). Jesus rebuked him. Philip was saying that he was willing to believe in God but God the Father was enough for him. Perhaps he didn't fully understand the implication of what he was saying because the very heart of the gospel message is that we need Jesus. It is Jesus who died on the Cross for our sins and rose again three days later. It is Jesus who opens the way to our heavenly Father through his death on the Cross.

It is a mistake to make up our own belief system. Philip was standing next to Jesus, the One who had been sent by God to declare salvation to the world. At that moment Philip was prepared to ignore all that Jesus was teaching him and declare that he was satisfied with his own understanding of God.

In a world of shifting values, our beliefs must be based on truth; otherwise our faith will be as effective and as lasting as building a fortress on sand. As Christians we believe in God as revealed in Scripture. He is God the Father, God the Son and God the Holy Spirit. Each person of the trinity is co-equal in power and glory. You cannot believe in God the Father and not believe in God the Son and God the Holy Spirit. It is Jesus who shows us the way to the Father and it is the Holy Spirit who enables us to live a new life of freedom and power. If we make up our own belief system where do we go when we need help and what do we find when we go there?

Many years ago I met two people, Ruth and John. Ruth was a Christian and was convinced that Jesus was the way, the truth and the life. Ruth met John, a young man who was not a Christian, nor was he convinced that what Jesus said was true. They fell in love. John declared his love for Ruth almost every day and asked her to be his girlfriend. Ruth did not return her love for John and refused to be his girlfriend – she was convinced that Jesus was the truth and the only way to God and everlasting life. Nevertheless, she prayed that John would come to know Jesus and become a Christian.

As friends, John would often accompany Ruth to church where he would listen to the pastor and have lively debates with him after the service. Everybody could see that John and Ruth were in love. But Ruth was determined that she would only marry someone who would be able to share her faith in Jesus. She was very wise.

One day, John was reading the newspaper and read about a man who had been found in the belly of a whale. He couldn't believe that this had really happened. One of his problems with the Bible was that he could not believe that the story of Jonah and the fish was true and, if that wasn't true, then maybe everything else in the Bible wasn't true. However, if, as reported in the newspaper, it was actually possible for a man to be in the belly of a whale and still be alive, then maybe other things in the Bible could be true as well. This was the turning point and John put his trust in Jesus and became a Christian. You can guess what happened next. Ruth was very happy to become

John's girlfriend and soon there was a wedding, which took place more than 21 years ago!

The four friends in Scripture put their trust in Jesus because they were convinced that he was their only hope for their friend. They were convinced and courageous.

Courageous

The Bible doesn't tell us the names of the four friends or even the name of the paralysed man. However, it was such a memorable occasion that it was included in Mark and Luke's gospel accounts of Jesus' life. These friends were very determined. We don't know how far they carried their friend on the mat, how hot it was that day or how difficult the journey. We know they arrived at the house and couldn't get in because Jesus was so popular that a great crowd had gathered to hear him teach. When the friends found that they couldn't get into the house they climbed up the stairs to the roof, still carrying their friend.

I wonder what the reaction of the people in the house would have been when they started to hear noises above them as the friends made a hole in the roof. Maybe bits of the roof started to fall onto the crowd below. When they began to lower the man on the mat down into the crowd there must have been a great commotion. All eyes looked up to the ceiling. I wonder how the friend felt as he was being lowered down. Perhaps a little worried! Imagine if that happened now – everybody would look up and wonder what was going to happen next. Maybe Jesus himself stopped talking and looked to see what was happening. Some people may have been annoyed because Jesus' teaching had been interrupted. Some people may have been anxious because they thought they were in danger. Others may have just been curious. What would your reaction have been? These friends persevered even though they may have been criticised. They were not thinking about themselves and this made them very bold and courageous.

Some people think that Christianity is boring. It can be if all we do is turn up to church each week and sing a few songs and say a few prayers. However, if you know Jesus then Christianity is never boring; it is exciting and life-changing. Jesus makes us bold and courageous. Jesus led me to Brazil – there is nothing boring about that! When you become a Christian you stop thinking about yourself and you start thinking about other people. Jesus came with a mission. It was a mission to bring salvation to the world – to rescue every person from the power of sin and guilt and bring freedom and love to all. When Jesus calls us to follow him he is asking us to join him in this mission.

I have a friend whose life is not boring. She was commissioned as a Salvation Army officer at the same time as I was. After working for a few years in North London and then Italy, she returned to the UK and was appointed as the director of Faith House, just across the road from Kings Cross railway station in London. She and a colleague officer walk around the area of Kings Cross late at night, talking with and reaching out to prostitutes, runaways and homeless people. This is the Midnight Patrol. During the day Faith House is open for people to come in and seek help.

What makes a person go on the Midnight Patrol? Why is my friend not afraid? She is convinced that Jesus is the only hope for the people she meets and it is Jesus who gives her the courage. In the area where she works there are several lap-dancing clubs and for many years she has wanted to reach out to the girls who work in those clubs. These girls are often trapped in a job that they may not have chosen. Some are tricked into it and find they cannot escape. Others got into the work because they needed the money. My friend had walked and prayed in the streets surrounding these clubs for more than two years. Finally she had her first breakthrough. She was invited into not just one, but two clubs. A new door was opened to her for God's work. Think about how much courage it took to sit in the manager's office of a lap-dancing club. That courage comes from Jesus.

This woman is not the only one breaking roofs so people can see Jesus. My husband and I have two friends who were born in Greece and came to the UK to be trained as officers. They were commissioned and worked for eight years in the UK. From the very moment that God called them to be officers they had a vision for The Salvation Army to have a presence in Greece. In 2008 they moved to Greece to begin that work. The husband works with the homeless, giving them food and finding them accommodation, and his wife ministers to girls who work in the sex industry. One year they helped seven girls leave their work to begin a new life. What makes them so courageous? This couple is convinced that Jesus is the Way, the Truth and the Life. They know that Jesus is the only hope for these girls and others they work with. Just like these present-day roof-breakers, the four friends in Scripture were convinced, courageous and had compassion.

Compassion

Jesus saw the paralysed man being lowered down through the roof and the Bible tells us that when he saw their faith he said, 'Son, your sins are forgiven' (Mark 2:5). Not only did Jesus heal the paralysed man but he also forgave his sins. When the religious people objected he asked them a question, 'Which is easier: to say to this paralysed man, "Your sins are forgiven", or to say, "Get up, take your mat and walk"?' (Mark 2:9). The truth is that if Jesus is the Son of God then he can do both. The crowd was amazed and said, 'We have never seen anything like this!' (Mark 2:12).

Let us think about that for a minute. Do we ever see miracles? We see miracles when we are convinced that Jesus is the way, the truth and the life. We see this kind of thing when we are courageous in the way we live our Christian lives. We see this kind of thing when we share the compassion of Jesus for people who need help. Where will your compassion take you? What roofs will you break to bring someone to Jesus?

Our son was very poorly when he was born. After 20 minutes of emergency care he was taken into the intensive care unit. Later a doctor came to speak to my husband and me while I was still in the delivery room. A new midwife had just started her shift and was tidying up the room. The doctor did not have good news for us.

When the doctor left the room the midwife, whose name was Patience, came over to me and said, 'You are Christians, aren't you?' And then she added, 'This is what the doctor says but God says different'. She took hold of our hands and prayed the most amazing prayer. She lifted up the name of Jesus and proclaimed him King of all Kings. She bowed her own knee in his presence and boldly came before his throne, asking for a miracle.

Twelve days later we took home a healthy baby. The doctors could not explain why our son had flatlined at birth or why he had not sustained any brain damage. We do not know why our baby survived while others do not. But we do know that we were taken to the feet of Jesus by a courageous and compassionate midwife who risked losing her job when she prayed that prayer. She was a roof-breaker!

Conclusion

The four friends in this story brought the paralysed man to Jesus to be healed. Their compassion for their friend led them to seek help. They were convinced that Jesus could and would help them and their conviction brought them courage. Jesus saw their faith and compassion and was moved to help the paralysed man. Their conviction, courage and compassion led them to become roof-breakers.

Where do you go when you need help? What do you put your trust in? Do you buy a lottery ticket hoping that one day you will win and everything will be fine? Some people go to fortune tellers or read their horoscopes to get help. Some people create their own belief system, thinking it enough to just believe in God. These are my questions for you. Are you convinced that Jesus is the way, the truth and the life? Are you convinced that Jesus has the power to heal people and to forgive sin? If you are convinced then you will live your life for him and he will give you the courage and compassion you need to become a roof-breaker. Roof-breakers don't worry about what people think of them. They are not concerned about their own reputation. Roof-breakers persevere in the face of criticism. Jesus welcomes roof-breakers; he sees that roof-breakers want to join him in mission to reach people.

If you would like to give your life to Jesus for the first time, here is a simple prayer that you can say: 'Father God, I repent of my sin. Forgive me through the blood of Jesus shed on the Cross. I am convinced that Jesus is the Way, the Truth and the Life. I put my trust in him today. Help me to live a new life. I receive your Holy Spirit and ask that he will teach and guide me each day. Amen.'

If you are already a Christian but have a renewed desire to be a roof-breaker for Jesus, here is a simple prayer:

Dear heavenly Father, I am convinced that Jesus is the Way, the Truth and the Life. I thank you for the work he has done and is doing in my life. Please give me the courage and compassion that I need in my present situation. Give me the courage and compassion that I need in order to go where you lead me. Help me to be a roof-breaker. Amen.

Colonel Naomi Lalngaihawmi
India Eastern Territory

The Word of God in Today's World

2 Timothy 3:14-17

Introduction

LET us consider and learn together about the Word of God in today's world. The Founder – William Booth – said, 'I want to see a new translation of the Bible into the hearts and conduct of living men and women. I want an improved translation – or transference it might be called – of the commandments and promises and teachings and influences of this book to the minds and feelings and words and activities of the men and women who hold on to it and swear by it and declare it to be an inspired book and the only authorised rule of life'.

What kind of world is the world in which we are living?

We live in a changing world. In spite of great developments, increased scientific knowledge, increased industrial production and greater wealth, the world we live in is in crisis. What do we see and hear from the printed and electronic media? Open a newspaper these days, listen to the news on the radio or television, and invariably you get the sense of trouble.

Our world is torn by strife – strife between political parties, strife between ethnic factions, and strife between nations. It is beset by problems – hunger, pollution of land and water, violence, increasing crime and over-crowded prisons. There are an alarming number of victims of drug and alcohol abuse, sex and human trafficking and suicide.

Looming over all is the threat of economic downturn, with widespread unemployment and material hardship. The under-developed and developing countries are in debt to the world banks with no prospect of ever being able to repay the loans. Nations are spending fantastic sums of money every year in creating the power to frighten and destroy because they cannot trust one another. War, genocide and terrorism happen and no one knows how to stop them. Meanwhile, the development of ever more terrifying nuclear weapons goes on. Morality is declining as corruption, sexual perversion, adultery, rape and theft happen more and more.

Is there a hope for us?

We have a hope! We have a hope for a better life here in this world and in the world to come because of Christ. Refer to 1 Corinthians 2:9, Philippians 3:20-21 and 2 Peter 3:13 to see evidence of this.

How should we behave in this kind of world?

Gilbert Ellis writes in his book *What a Hope!* that because of our hope for the future, a hope which says that what we are and do in this life will influence the world to come and our place in it, we must not neglect the world in which we dwell, or our body which is the temple of the living God. The apostle Peter urges us to 'make every effort to be found spotless, blameless and at peace with him' (2 Peter 3:14).

Authority of the Bible

We believe that the Scriptures of the Old and New Testaments were given by inspiration of God, and that they only constitute the Divine rule of Christian faith and practice (Article 1, *The Doctrines of The Salvation Army*).

There are different ideas and values in today's world. What was not right in the eyes of people in the past is becoming right in the eyes of people today. In the midst of conflicting ideas, opinions and values, the Word of God should be the source and measuring rod for us to know what is right and wrong and how we should live and behave.

Samuel Logan Brengle in his book *Helps to Holiness* writes of the Bible, 'The Bible is God's recipe book for making holy people. You must follow the recipe exactly, if you want to be a holy, Christ-like person.'

'The Word of God has dynamic application to our life and our relationship to the world around us. We derive from the Bible not only information, but also inspiration; not only enlightenment, but also enrichment. We need not only to penetrate the Word, but also to personalise it, for it becomes not only revelational but also relational' (*Discipleship – Vision and Mission* edited by Edward Read).

Mother Teresa said, 'Know the Word of God, love the Word of God, live the Word of God and give the Word of God.' This saying is true because, 'All Scripture is God-breathed and is useful for teaching, rebuking, correcting and training in righteousness, so that the servant of God may be thoroughly equipped for every good work' (2 Timothy 3:16-17).

It is the Word of God that our dear Army Mother (Catherine Booth) wanted to share when she said, 'William, I want to say a word', leading to her first public sermon later that evening.

May God help us all to live the Word of God in today's world.

Major Karin Larsson
Sweden and Latvia Territory

Forgiveness and Salvation – the Start of a Holy Life

Acts 4:12 NKJV

Nor is there salvation in any other, for there is no other name under Heaven given among men by which we must be saved.

Acts 10:43 NKJV

To him all the prophets witness that, through his name, whoever believes in him will receive remission of sins.

Ephesians 1:7-11 NKJV

In him we have redemption through his blood, the forgiveness of sins, according to the riches of his grace which he made to abound toward us in all wisdom and prudence, having made known to us the mystery of his will, according to his good pleasure which he purposed in himself, that in the dispensation of the fullness of the times he might gather together in one all things in Christ, both which are in Heaven and which are on Earth – in him. In him also we have obtained an inheritance, being predestined according to the purpose of him who works all things according to the counsel of his will.

Introduction

MARY takes a welcome rest in the shadow under the outhouse roof. The work on the farm has been hectic during the last several weeks and everyone has been busy. The crops have been harvested and Mary knows that all has gone well. Before the weekend it will be finished for this season. From around the country rumours have been heard about drought, crop failure and famine. She has listened when the men have spoken about it and once again she can thank God for sparing her family. She couldn't begin to think what might have happened if the Lord had not shown them mercy.

Mary looks out over the farm from the shelter of the shade. She catches sight of the people who have become part of her life. Far away she sees David. As always, he fills her with pride and love. She has known David as long as she can remember. He is a good father to their children, and well respected in the community. Many thoughts go through her mind during her short rest.

They say that your whole life can pass in your mind in just a few moments. That is what Mary experiences right now. Seeing the beautiful woman standing there, you cannot know what is hidden in her thoughts or all the different feelings in her heart.

She thinks about 'the secret'. Most of the people near her have repressed or forgotten it. No one talks about it any longer, though it is still there, all the time. Mary fears that 'the secret' is what is eating David on the inside. In the beginning, a long time ago, she noticed how he had changed and she tried to talk to him about it but he became either cold and silent or fell into a fit of rage.

Now she doesn't want to risk it any more but almost every night she wakes up to hear David talking in his sleep. Rarely can she discern words and phrases from his dreams. Sometimes it seems as if Grandfather – at least that is what everybody calls her father-in- law – and David speak about 'it' for a long time in the dreams, and the words she hears frequently are 'Why?', 'Forget him' and 'Please, forgive me!' Sometimes her sleeping husband sounds like a small unhappy child, saying 'Please, come home Simon! I beg you, please, come home again!' Or 'Please, father, forgive me, forgive me!'

Sometimes Mary tries to console David but that is not easy when she doesn't even know the name of the sorrow, anxiety and anger of her beloved husband.

As for Grandfather, the fact that every evening since it happened he walks to the road as if he is looking for someone who never comes, doesn't bother them any longer. As a matter of fact, he is getting much older now, and doesn't always talk in his right senses. Let him be; he does no harm with his daydreams!

Well daydreaming is what Mary herself is giving way to in the cool shadow by the wall. Suddenly she is called back to reality. What is that noise? Has something happened? Why is everyone running around like a hen on a hot griddle? What are they screaming? What does she hear? She doesn't dare believe her ears: 'He's come back! He's come back!' Even if she has a deep inner feeling of what it might be, she can't decide whether the words they are screaming are good news or the beginning of a catastrophe. Can it be true? Where is David?

I took the liberty of placing Mary in the story Jesus told to help people understand that each person is much loved and highly valued by God. It is a story about an ordinary family that is an illustration of the necessity of forgiveness and salvation. It may appear difficult to believe but, when you experience it, forgiveness is a glorious and life-changing gift from God.

Jesus told the parable that is recorded in Luke's Gospel chapter 15. The younger of two sons nagged his father until he was given his heritage. While his father was still alive the son wasted the entire amount. What a shame and dishonour! He became miserably poor, destitute and was filled with repentance, longing for home. Before it was too late he came to his senses and returned home.

Maybe it is not difficult for any of us to identify with his situation when the young man thought about what to say to his father if he dared to return home: 'Father, I have sinned before God and you, and I am no longer worthy to be called your son. But, please, let me work as one of your servants.' That was his simple prayer.

The story ends in a remarkable way. A great celebration took place where the younger brother, the squanderer, is the principal figure and there is great joy as the boy, once thought dead, returns.

But the older brother could not, would not, take part in the happiness. Maybe we too can identify with his angry way of thinking! 'Daddy, I can tell you, I have always…and he, I can tell you, has never…and you, Dad, should at least… All the years I have been working here without…!'

When we listen to a story from the Bible, we see ourselves in the characters. The story and the people can mirror another time in another culture but we can recognise ourselves. We also hope that there is forgiveness and salvation for us. We also hope that 'the secret' in our lives, through the grace of God, can be exposed, the sin forgiven and the sinner saved. In different ways, all of the characters, just like all of us, need to ask for forgiveness.

We may also be thinking about what we could say to our Father if we dared to go back home to ask for grace and mercy. Why is it so difficult to believe that our Father could be standing there, happy, welcoming and embracing us when we come?

I can cheat myself by thinking I do not have to, but in fact all of us have to ask for forgiveness. Trying to live without forgiveness from people and from God is really a poor way of living. And what relief and freedom there is in receiving and giving forgiveness!

'For all have sinned and fall short of the glory of God, being justified freely by his grace through the redemption that is in Christ Jesus' (Romans 3:23-24 *NKJV*). When I was a small girl I began to steal coins from my father's piggy bank. I can assure you I felt almost paralysed with shame and guilt when I understood what I had done, and I had to tell my father, in spite of the expected consequences.

I can recall the moment my father taught me what forgiveness is – forgiveness before men and forgiveness before God. I confessed my theft and there was no doubt about my repentance. What an unforgettable relief when my father said the life-changing words, 'I forgive you, my daughter. We shall also ask the Lord about forgiveness and I am quite sure that this will never happen again!' What a picture, from real life, of what forgiveness and salvation is!

You are the one who knows what forgiveness looks like in your life. You are the only one who knows. You know which person or persons you have to forgive or ask forgiveness from.

Your Father, God himself, is waiting there for you to come. He is standing right here with forgiveness, salvation and a holy life ready to give it to you. You don't have to worry about what to say and what to do! Why not try the way so many have done in the past? Kneel at the mercy seat or right where you are, and your life will be changed with just two words, 'Father, forgive'.

Yes, Jesus! Yes, Jesus!

Colonel Edith Löfgren
Sweden and Latvia Territory

Quite Intrusive
Luke 11:1-10, Psalm 13

JESUS was asked to give a lesson in how to pray. His disciples asked, 'Lord, teach us to pray' (Luke 11:1). This was an interesting question and an interesting wish. Why did they not ask, 'Lord, teach us to preach'? After all, Jesus was a superb preacher and the art of speech was very highly regarded at that time. Just imagine getting some good tips from such a successful speaker!

Neither did they ask, 'Lord, teach us to perform miracles', as there were so many unusual things that happened around Jesus that created commotion among people. It would be so helpful to know how to perform miracles. But what the disciples wanted, and what they asked was, 'Lord, teach us to pray'. So many times they had seen with their own eyes how fundamentally important prayer was for Jesus, and that prayer was why so many things happened.

Jesus was a very social person. He walked around among the people. He took part in parties and celebrations. He had very public activities and was often surrounded by large crowds. He helped and healed so many people – his 'social work' among people was really significant. But it was also very important to him to go aside for prayer. The disciples had noticed that. They understood that Jesus had a special contact with his heavenly Father through prayer, and this was also from where he got power, inspiration and guidance. His work would not have functioned without it, so that is why the disciples wanted to know more about the secret of

125

prayer. And they did not need to ask twice. Immediately Jesus gave them a lesson in the subject.

As a good teacher, Jesus starts his lesson with some sentences for the disciples to learn by heart – the Lord's Prayer, which Christians around the world still pray. So this part of the lesson was very well taught.

Then Jesus tells them a story with a clear point and a challenge and concludes with a promise that tells us where it all leads.

The story is about a man who had visitors arrive at his house in the middle of the night. He had nothing to offer them to eat and the larder was empty. This was a very embarrassing situation in that culture. Generosity towards visitors was a matter of honour for them.

What does he do? He walks over to his neighbour's house and pounds eagerly on the door, even though it is the middle of the night. He says, 'Friend, lend me three loaves of bread; a friend of mine on a journey has come to me, and I have no food to offer him' (vv 5-6). Eventually, after quite some persuasion, a drowsy person opens the door and gives him what he wanted.

What is the point that Jesus wants to make clear with this story? Jesus tells us that this man gets what he needs because he is so intrusive and eager. The man really was intrusive, because at that time most houses were built with only one room. The whole family slept on the floor in that same room close to each other to keep warm. If one got up, the rest of the family would surely wake up too. And not only the family, but also the animals that quite often lived in the same room – goats, hens, cocks, mules, and so on. So, if one of the family got up, the hens would start clucking, the cock perhaps would crow, the children might start crying and the noise would spoil everyone's sleep.

The point is very clear. Jesus wants us to be persevering in our prayers. He is speaking about being tireless about what is important in our prayer.

Today there are many different ideas concerning prayer: you should sit correctly, breathe right, think right, hold up your hands, read out loud in a monotonous voice, even jump or fall backwards.

It was not this kind of behaviour that opened the door for the man in the story. Jesus does not teach or mention one word about such behaviour.

His teaching is all about genuineness and having pure hearts. These are the only things that matter in this context.

Problems and difficulties can drive us to desperation or resignation, but can also drive us into a deeper life of prayer, and important things happen to us then. Problems and difficulties can sometimes help us to see things from another perspective and we are able to see that a door opens for us. We do not always get what we have asked for, but we receive as much as we need, just like the man in the story.

As we read in Luke 11:1-10, the challenge for us is to be bold in prayer and really trust that the Lord knows all about our needs. It is good to remember that he knows our deepest thoughts, even those that we are unable to put into words.

The promise is that we will find if we seek, a door will be opened if we knock.

Psalm 13 is a bold prayer when life is hard. We can see the despair in the first part, and we can also see how the psalmist 'knocks on the door'. I like the conclusion of this psalm; it is like seeing 'the door' being opened:

How long, Lord?
Will you forget me forever?
How long will you hide your face from me?
How long must I wrestle with my thoughts
And day after day have sorrow in my heart?
How long will my enemy triumph over me?

Look on me and answer, Lord my God.
Give light to my eyes, or I will sleep in death,
And my enemy will say, 'I have overcome him',
And my foes will rejoice when I fall.

But I trust in your unfailing love;
My heart rejoices in your salvation.
I will sing the Lord's praise,
For he has been good to me.

Commissioner Gudrun Lydholm
Denmark Territory

Calvary Questions

Mark 15:33-37

THE word 'why' might be the word most frequently used in our lives. Why did I do that? Why did I say this? Or why did he/she do that? These questions belong to our everyday life and will face us on many days.

Small children might not be able to utter many words, but the word 'why' will soon be part of their vocabulary. Why is the sky blue? Why does the dog bark? Why does this man have a funny nose? Why are you angry with me? Why have all the leaves gone from the trees? The 'why' questions go in all directions as the child tries to find meaning and order in life's mysteries. The questions reach out to material things, towards the weather and nature, towards people and animals. Parents will hear this 'why' through childhood and youth.

And it doesn't stop there – we all pose the question 'why', not only the everyday 'why', but the deeper 'whys'. Sometimes we ask it in surprise and even wonder; sometimes in expectation or in joy. At other times the 'why' grows out of pain and the accompanying isolation.

Often in these situations there is no answer. The question stays in the air and grows bigger and more difficult to handle. At other times we try to get an answer which might satisfy us for a while and make it possible for us to go on with life.

The 'why' out of pain
This is the sort of question screamed out of pain. Jesus cried out on the Cross 'Why?' The question seemed to stay in the air. It lingered around

129

the Cross. It is still there today. Yet we do not have a real or satisfying answer. We can try to find one, but it might never satisfy us completely. The gospel does not try to give an answer. The question is allowed to stay there in all its cruelty and forsakenness.

Even though we might not be able to find a satisfying answer, we cannot help trying to find one. Christians through the centuries have tried to give an answer to this 'why'. I remember as a teenager of 13 or 14 years of age, on my first Easter Bible camp, I asked the question: 'Why did Jesus feel that God had forsaken him?' The teacher answered me that in this moment Jesus bore the sins of the world. All that terrible sin separated him from God, and that was why he cried out. I accepted the answer for the time being. The teacher was an older officer, so I accepted his greater wisdom, but not for long. The answer did not really satisfy me. Since then I have continued to try to find an answer, but never really succeeded.

I am sure many of us continue in the same way to find the answer that satisfies us. While we are seeking meaning in the pain and forsakenness, it is important to note who is asked, and who the question is directed to. Let's look further.

The 'why' is directed to my God. It is not a 'why' shouted into the blue. In the 'why' there is a conviction, a deep-seated trust that my God is there, that he can and does hear the cry of pain, the question of pain. In the midst of suffering, pain, despair and forsakenness God is maintained as my God. That has not altered. In the midst of the despair, the pain and bewilderment, it is an exclamation of faith and trust.

In a dialogue with God or in prayer time under normal circumstances the words might have fallen in this way: 'You are my God, and I do not understand why you have left me alone and isolated in the midst of this horrible situation.' But it is not a time of meditation. The 'why' which is cried out from the Cross is the cry of torture, the cry of pain, the cry of loneliness – there is neither room nor time for reflection, only this 'why', which cries out the terrible pain.

It is when our cry to God expresses our whole existence, when the emptiness and the loneliness seem to be total, that God is closest. It is only in the Gospels of Matthew and Mark that the account of this 'why' of pain is recorded.

We might have known this feeling of godforsakenness personally – a feeling of being totally alone, a sense of isolation and emptiness. Perhaps we have cried out 'Why have you forsaken me?' We might have cried it out into seeming total emptiness. Or we have been able to combine our 'why' with the words 'My God, my God'. When we are able to do that – when we are able to direct our questions to him – then we are crying our pain and isolation out to a presence, even though we might feel there is only emptiness and godforsakenness around us. Underneath our despair we know that God is out there.

The message of Good Friday

The profound message of Good Friday is that God is my God. That he is my God personally. That is truth for each human being. He is not a distant or remote God, and we can claim him as 'my God'.

Jesus cried out his 'Why?'; he lived through the feelings of emptiness and godforsakenness but he crossed over from life to death. Because he did that, the message of Good Friday, the message of Easter, is that we never need to do that on our own. We never need to do this in isolation and loneliness. Jesus has gone before us. There will always be a presence of 'my God' for each of us, a presence of him, who once went through the darkness, the pain, the hopelessness and the godforsakenness. The proclamation of Easter morning, the amazing message of the Resurrection, that comes so fresh to us through the pages of the gospels in spite of 2,000 years distance – this message guarantees this presence for each of us during all situations in life.

Another 'why'

There may be other 'whys' which confront us. It might be a painful 'why' coming to us in times of reflection or remorse. Then our questions may be: 'My God, my God why have I forsaken you? Why did I distance myself from your presence? Why did I distance myself from your will? Why did I distance myself from your commandments? Why did I prefer

131

meaninglessness, when you were there offering meaning and purpose in life? Why did I prefer to be cast here and there, when you could give direction and goals for my life?'

The only one who can give an honest answer to these questions is the one asking them. We might even pose the questions already knowing the answers. But the questions are important, because in the very questions there is an exclamation of faith, however feeble the faith is. They are directed to 'my God'. In the questions there is hope that things will be different and, I think, there is a knowledge that things can be different. The satisfying answers for these questions do exist. The answers come from the Cross. They come from the prayer of the Crucified: 'Father, forgive them, for they do not know what they are doing' (Luke 23:34).

That prayer still stands today and is uttered on our behalf, as it has been uttered since the day of crucifixion when Jesus prayed this prayer in the midst of pain and agony.

May God help us to pose these questions and receive his forgiveness. May God bless each of us. Amen.

Major Jenine Main
*United Kingdom Territory with
the Republic of Ireland*

Rescue Me

Psalm 40:1-3

IMAGINE a young girl with short, straight hair, dressed in jeans and trainers, always climbing trees or playing football with the boys. This was me when I was nine years old. I lived by a playing field where I regularly went to play football. Most of the boys I played with were friends of my older brother and all of them were a couple of years older than me. Although my brother always objected to me being there, it seemed his friends didn't mind – you see, I was good! They always picked me for their team.

One day after playing football the boys dared me to climb on to the roof of the club changing rooms. It was a flat-roofed building about 12 feet high. Not one to ever refuse a challenge, I climbed up. I can't quite remember how I actually got up there, but I clearly remember being unable to get down – and none of the boys was big enough to help me. My brother eventually had to get our father to help. Dad was not impressed. I was in big trouble! However, I was glad to be rescued, and never climbed up again.

Many of us would have 'rescue' stories to tell. Perhaps they involve floods, accidents or even large dogs! But what about those situations that may not be life threatening, yet still make us feel like we are in need of rescue – broken relationships, low self-esteem, grief, financial difficulties, unemployment? How many people are crying out to be rescued because they feel trapped by their circumstances?

133

Psalm 40:1-3 *NCV* clearly tells us that God is in the business of rescuing people. 'I waited patiently for the Lord. He turned to me and heard my cry. He lifted me out of the pit of destruction, out of the sticky mud. He stood me on a rock and made my feet steady. He put a new song in my mouth, a song of praise to our God. Many people will see this and worship him. Then they will trust the Lord.'

How brilliant to know that God wants to reach down and rescue us from the situations we find ourselves in. His desire is to turn our circumstances around, to lift us out of the depths of despair, to stand us on a firm rock and give us a new song – not a song of despair or gloom, but one of praise to our God.

How does God do this? Let's take a look at God's work through history – how he has rescued people since the creation of the world. Here are some examples:

In Genesis, God placed Joseph in a position of high authority where he could rescue his family from famine. In Exodus the Israelites had become slaves to the Egyptians and God sent Moses to save them. In the book of Esther, God placed Esther in the king's court 'for such a time as this' – to save the Jewish people from certain death.

In the book of Daniel, Shadrach, Meshach and Abednego were thrown into the furnace because they refused to worship Nebuchadnezzar's gold statue, and God rescued them from the flames. God kept Daniel safe in the lions' den.

In the New Testament, God sent Jesus to rescue the world! 'For God so loved the world that he gave his one and only Son, that whoever believes in him shall not perish but have eternal life' (John 3:16).

God rescued Peter from prison and Paul from being shipwrecked, beaten and stoned.

These people were all stuck in a pit of some kind, and all needed to be rescued. Many of us have found ourselves in difficult, desperate, even dangerous situations when we too needed help. The good news is that God is willing to reach down and pull us out of these situations and set our feet on solid ground.

In his earthly ministry Jesus rescued people – from physical and mental illness, from low self-esteem and from humdrum, ordinary existences. But he also rescued people from their sin, from Satan, and from death itself.

Mary Magdalene was one such person Jesus rescued. It is often thought that Mary Magdalene was a prostitute, although there is no Scripture that says this. We do read that Jesus saved Mary from seven demons (Luke 8:2). What those demons were, we are not told. But once she was free, we know that Mary was so devoted to Christ that she helped support his ministry out of her own means (Luke 8:1-3).

Mary was devoted to Jesus until the end and was one of the women at the foot of the Cross. She was first at the tomb and discovered the stone rolled away. Once she was completely in darkness. Jesus saved her and she became a follower.

Jesus did indeed rescue Mary. He heard her cry, lifted her out of the 'sticky mud' of her life and stood her on a firm place. Possibly trapped in a cycle of self-destruction, Mary's self-esteem and self-image must have been rock bottom, yet still Jesus reached out to her. He stretched out his hand and offered her his love and forgiveness.

This didn't mean that from then on Mary's life would have been all stars and roses! Although the Bible doesn't say so, I imagine it would have been hard for her to leave her old life behind. Hard for her to accept complete forgiveness and look at herself in a brand new way. But Jesus did this for her. Even so, she would have experienced loss, grief and pain when the one who had given her everything was taken away. Jesus' death and burial would have seemed like the end. Did she feel lost again? Did she think that once more she had nothing, that she was just a nobody?

Jesus came once again to rescue her from these doubts and feelings. Imagine the desperation Mary must have felt seeing the tomb empty, her Saviour's body presumed stolen. Yet God sent angels to comfort her, and then Jesus showed himself to her. Mary was the first to see Jesus following his resurrection, and he reached out yet again to save her from her feelings of loss. Mary must have experienced the words of Psalm 40 all over again; there would have been a new song in her mouth, a song of praise to her God.

These rescue situations didn't only happen in Bible times. Sarah (not her real name) walked into our church one Sunday. She returned for subsequent visits, and slowly began to confide in me about her situation. She and her husband had lived abroad for a number of years and had a villa in Europe. Unfortunately her husband, who was in his late 50s, had recently died. Sarah was a strong, self-sufficient lady and on the surface appeared to be handling the situation well, but underneath she was struggling to get out of the depths of grief and loss – the loss of her husband, the loss of her future life abroad and the loss of a long and happy retirement with her life's partner. Sarah was depressed, she didn't think life was worth living and she had nothing to look forward to. The loss of her husband had taken away any sense of purpose or direction. She was stuck in a pit, and didn't know how to get out.

As she continued to attend our church she realised that God was interested in her. More than that – God loved her, and wanted to reach out to her and rescue her from the depths of despair. Praise God that Sarah accepted the strong rescuing arm of God. She found a new, full life, and eventually went abroad to serve God in a small, deprived community. God had put a new song of praise in her mouth.

There are many situations people need to be rescued from. Being nine years old and stuck on a roof is one thing, but some people face threatening, abusive or addictive situations, while others live with difficult relationships, destructive behaviour or harmful friendships. Whatever the situation, God is willing to reach down and rescue us. If we do as the psalmist says and wait patiently, God will hear our cry and lift us out of our 'pit of destruction', out of the 'sticky mud' and stand us on a rock, making us steady and firm. God himself is that rock; the one who can give us strength and security in the knowledge of his faithfulness and unconditional love.

What a difference God can make to our lives. We can be saved – Jesus has done this for us and wants us to experience it for ourselves. What difference would it make to your life if you knew there was someone reaching out to pull you up out of your own personal pit, out of the circumstances you find yourself in? God has a history of doing this; he has done it before, he will do it again – and he can do it for you.

Major Liliana Makagiantang
Indonesia Territory

Human Weakness Equals Perfection in God

2 Corinthians 12:1-10

WE cannot deny that in this life there are times when we experience struggles and challenges. There are times when the refreshing winds cure our souls and we feel life is wonderful. But there are also times when the storms come into our lives and make us waver in our faith.

That day, for me, was Wednesday 12 August 2009. When I woke that morning, nothing was unusual. Morning routines and family quiet time ran normally. At 6.30am I came downstairs from the bedroom to the office, and everything changed. Suddenly I felt an unbearable pain in my left side. I had never experienced such pain before and it became more intense as it spread through my body.

At the hospital I met with the surgeon and kidney specialist. As a result of tests and the CT scan, surgery would be necessary, possibly to remove one kidney. On hearing this news, I felt no shock or fear. From the beginning of the pain I had prayed and had surrendered to the will of God. I was surrounded as well with prayer support and visits from people who loved me. It was planned that I would have the surgery on the Friday. Unfortunately, because my blood haemoglobin had dropped, blood transfusions were given and surgery was rescheduled for Saturday morning, 15 August. Once again surgery had to be delayed as I was taken by an ambulance to another hospital with specialised equipment. Once there, I was prepared for surgery.

During the hours of waiting, I felt some moments of uncertainty. Why? Because so many people were praying different prayers. Some prayed that the surgery would not be necessary, while others prayed for God to bless the operation – that all equipment to be used would be purified, that God would provide wisdom to the surgeons and that God would guide the decisions made during surgery. 'Which prayer would the Lord allow?' I wondered to myself.

In the end, when I was taken to the operating room, I prayed that God's will would be done. I was singing in my heart a verse of a song, 'In this time my power is helpless, your power is perfect'. The words continued until I lost consciousness but I was strengthened and assured that his power would work perfectly.

After regaining consciousness, I faintly heard the doctor explain to my husband that the left kidney had been removed. The pain that I felt was very unusual but it did not make me despair because I remembered that the power of God is certainly greater than the pain, and that he was also able to help me recover more quickly than the medicines I had to take while in the ICU for several days. Every second on the clock that I saw on the wall made me grateful to God who had given me an opportunity to live.

I am grateful for the attention, visits and prayer support from my family, friends, church members, officers and employees. It has changed everything. I'm now strong; I no longer remember the pain and can only remember all the goodness of God.

Within one week after the surgery I could go to church to worship, grateful for all the things that I experienced, and I could even stand on the platform to testify.

The next day, I was able to lead activities in the hospital service. The doctor considered my recovery as 'very fast'. Normally, patients with similar surgery could only move around after three months. One doctor said that I was very strong but I told him that I was not strong. I believe in God and prayer support from people who constantly prayed for me. Another doctor said my life was a miracle.

The apostle Paul also experienced struggles and challenges, both in his physical body as well as his circumstances. He said that he was given a 'thorn in the flesh'. For this struggle he had prayed to God to take away this 'thorn in the flesh', but God said, 'My grace is sufficient for you, for my power is made perfect in weakness' (2 Corinthians 12:7-9).

From my experiences and from the testimonies of the apostle Paul, we get some spiritual lessons. When we are weak and helpless, God assures that his power is perfect even in the midst of 'storm'.

'For you have delivered me from death and my feet from stumbling, that I may walk before God in the light of life' (Psalm 56:13). 'Yes, my soul, find rest in God; my hope comes from him' (Psalm 62:5).

When sickness strikes or we experience bad things, remember the goodness of God. Certainly his grace is greater than the difficulties we face and because of that we remain strong and are always grateful in any difficult situation.

We must realise that we do not need to understand everything that is happening in our lives; we need to know that God is always there in every situation we experience. 'Even though I walk through the darkest valley, I will fear no evil, for you are with me...' (Psalm 23:4).

From this experience I was taught about the miracles of God with a different understanding. Miracles are not just something that can happen when we pray to God to change our circumstances. Miracles often happen when God gives us the ability to pass through the hardship – a life that does not conform with our requests to God but what the Lord gives us for our own good.

Even though my body is not perfect anymore, I can still carry out my ministry responsibilities properly. I realise that it is the power of God. 'Therefore I will boast all the more gladly about my weaknesses, so that Christ's power may rest on me' (2 Corinthians 12:9).

Friends, I do not know what situation in life you are in right now or the trials and weaknesses you are experiencing. Whatever the 'storms' you are facing, believe that at times like these you may know the power of God is perfect.

When we have been through these experiences in our weakness, we find the perfection of God. Then we know the perfect work of the Lord. Hallelujah!

'But as for me, it is good to be near God. I have made the Sovereign Lord my refuge; I will tell of all your deeds' (Psalm 73:28).

Captain Wilma L. Mason
USA Southern Territory

Walk of Holiness

Ephesians 5:1-21

WHILE waiting for the return of his mother, the three-year-old boy sat next to his father in the airport lobby. In an effort to entertain his son, the father handed the child a storybook. As the child grew still, several bystanders noticed he was reading his book just as the father was reading the newspaper. Sitting side by side with their legs crossed, there was no denying their relationship, but something was distinctly different. Upon closer examination it was noticed the child's book was being held upside down! The child had a strong desire to be just like his father; he just did not know exactly how to accomplish his desires.

In the New Testament book of Ephesians we find this same situation with the church of Ephesus. The church desired an intimate relationship with God, but it needed coaching on how to bring this desire to fruition. In an effort to continue disciplining the church, Paul, imprisoned in Rome, sent a circular letter which reminded it that God himself chose it for a life of holiness: 'For he chose us in him before the creation of the world to be holy and blameless in his sight. In love he predestined us to be adopted as his sons [and daughters] through Jesus Christ' (Ephesians 1:4-5 *NIV 1984*).

In Ephesians chapter five, Paul challenges the church with the steps necessary, both then and now, to move from meandering along the road of life to that of purposefully walking the journey God himself has designed.

In an effort for us to be like our heavenly Father, 'Be imitators of God' (Ephesians 5:1 *NIV 1984*), we are challenged to walk in three distinct ways: walk in love, walk in light and walk in wisdom.

Walk in love

Walking in love is more than telling someone you love them. The worldly culture in which we live has eroded the word 'love' to the point of distraction. For most, love is merely a verb describing how we feel about everything. We love ice cream, we love a particular dress and we love the colour that was chosen for our walls. This love is noncommittal and will change when the newest flavours, styles or colours are introduced to the public. This is not so of the love described in chapter five. Godly love is an action. Godly love is powerful, persevering and persuasive.

Powerful love can transform the very heart of who you are. Ephesians 5:2 says, 'and live a life of love, just as Christ loved us and gave himself up for us as a fragrant offering and sacrifice to God'. The love that God had for us, his finest creation, was one that sacrificed his Son so that we could be reconciled to him. Without this sacrifice we would have no way to dwell in the presence of our creator. It was through this act of love that our lives have the possibility of transformation. We will be a true reflection of the love of God when we can love others the way he chose to love us. This life of holiness will allow us to dwell in his holy presence.

Persevering love can reach even the most obstinate of souls. Can we be so foolish as to believe we wholeheartedly responded the first time Jesus knocked upon our heart's door? Scripture reminds us, 'Here I am [says Jesus]! I stand at the door and knock. If anyone hears my voice and opens the door, I will come in and eat with that person, and they with me' (Revelation 3:20). As imitators of God we are called to exhibit a love that never gives up on the unsaved. This is holy living, in that we give of ourselves for the salvation of others.

Persuasive love can speak to the heart and minds of God's children. Bringing others into the knowledge of the saving grace of Jesus Christ is our only mission as children of God. 'Therefore go and make disciples of all nations, baptising them in the name of the Father and of the Son and of the Holy Spirit, and teaching them to obey everything I have commanded you' (Matthew 28:19-20).

Persuasive love can convey the urgent need for a life change. Persuasive love can bring about a life change that will move the listener from living outside the realms of salvation to that of walking with God in his holiness. Being imitators of God means we must learn to share God's love in a manner which will reach the minds of the intellect and the hearts of the practical.

When we have learned to walk in love we must then learn how to walk in light.

Walk in light

In verses eight to ten Paul reminds us as dearly loved children of God that we are to walk continuously in light – the light of Christ. Paul is clear to remind the church of the sins found in this world which work quickly to ensnare us: greed, sexual immorality, foolish talk, obscenity, disobedience, idolatry and deceptive people. In Ephesians 5:7 he gives a stern warning with regard to befriending these sins, 'Therefore do not be partners with them.'

Can you remember a time when you were afraid of the dark? The kind of fear that has your heart pounding, your pulse racing and you can hardly catch your breath. Now think for a moment – what exactly were you afraid was going to happen? Truth be told, most would say they were scared of the unknown. The things that hide in the dark are most likely the origins of our fears. In reflecting upon sin and the craftiness of Satan there is a great deal of validity to our fears.

It should be no surprise that Satan is called the prince and ruler of darkness. It is in this darkness that his evil deeds can be kept in secret. While Satan is referred to as the prince of darkness, Jesus is boldly called the Light of the World. As children of God it is said in Matthew 5:14, 'You are the light of the world'.

When Jesus returns to sweep us up to be with him in paradise he will bring forth a light that will quickly expose the evil deeds of the world for what they are – sin that separates us from God. Paul urgently pleads with those who are either lost in the sins of the world or who are experimenting with the sins of the world in the following words: '…Wake up, sleeper, rise from the dead, and Christ will shine on you' (Ephesians 5:14).

As children of God we cannot be caught sleeping in our sins. To be an imitator of Christ Jesus we have to walk as children of God. We have to be free from the sins that would enslave our souls. When we walk as children of love and children of light then we are becoming true reflections of our Father God.

The final way that Paul encourages us to walk is that of wisdom.

Walk in wisdom

When people want to draw our attention away from foolish decisions to wise ones they will often remind us of the old saying, 'using your head for more than a hatrack'. In verses 15-21 Paul encourages the people of Ephesus to remember those things they have been taught from the time of their conversion to now. They have to take what they know and apply it to the decisions they make when faced with the temptation to fall back into a sinful life. Verse 17 says, 'Therefore do not be foolish, but understand what the Lord's will is'. The Lord's will is that you and I would choose to be reconciled to him by the blood that was provided in the death of Jesus Christ on the Cross.

Making wise decisions is not instinctive. In order to make a wise decision we must first understand the problem – sin. Secondly, we must be aware of our options: choosing a life in Christ, which equals eternal life and peace, or choosing a life in Satan, which leads to eternal death and destruction.

Lastly, we have to commit to our choice. In Revelation chapter three we read of a church (Laodicea) desiring to engage in activities of the world and claiming to serve our holy God. Jesus boldly tells them in verse 16, 'So, because you are lukewarm – neither hot nor cold – I am about to spit you out of my mouth'.

Paul's intention for writing this letter to the church of Ephesus was to encourage the new converts in their daily walk with God. It is because of our adoption into the family of God that we enjoy the great privilege of dwelling in the very presence of our heavenly Father. The longer we dwell in the presence of our Father the more like him we will become. It is in this 'dwelling' that we are able to reflect our Father. Just as the child in the airport who loved his father was a reflection of the one he loved, we too will reflect the one (God) whom we love and adore.

Major Elsa Oalang
The Philippines Territory

The *I Ams* of John the Baptist

John 1:19-37

THE world has its own definitions and descriptions of greatness. For military types, greatness is heroism and patriotism. For those in education, greatness is found in the long lists of scholarly achievements attached to a person's name. For those in the field of the arts, greatness is equivalent to the sounds of classical music and the beauty found in museums and art galleries. For those in the field of entertainment, greatness has given birth to the cult of the celebrity.

However, Jesus chose an obscure character to describe greatness in the context of the Kingdom of God. He said in Matthew 11:11, 'Truly I tell you, among those born of women there has not risen anyone greater than John the Baptist; yet whoever is least in the Kingdom of Heaven is greater than he.'

What made John the Baptist great? He may be peculiar because he was born when his parents were very old and his father lost his voice as a result of doubting what he considered impossible good news (Luke 1:5-20). He may be bizarre because he lived in the wilderness, wore clothes made of camel's hair and ate locusts and wild honey as his staple food (Matthew 3:4). He may be extraordinary because, although he was as rugged as the wilderness, he won followers and people came to be baptised by him. He may have died a martyr's death because he stood for what was right. Having said all this, there must be something about John that deserved the remark from Jesus.

147

As the forerunner of the Messiah, John exemplified how a servant of God should fulfil his or her mission on Earth. At the turning point of his ministry, John made at least three important claims. This message will centre on the great *I ams* of John and how every claim reveals the character of a truly great servant of God.

When asked about his true identity John replied, '*I am* not the Messiah' (John 1:20). I am here for a reason and a season.

John could have claimed greatness equal to the Messiah. People thought he was Elijah, the great prophet. He had his own followers who called him 'Rabbi' (John 3:26). The word 'rabbi' came from a Semitic root word meaning 'great' or 'head'. In a society where many professed to have been the saviour of Israel, John could have made the same claim.

On the contrary, John had no problem of identity and worth. He knew himself and his mission. As the forerunner of Christ, he knew that he was bound to time and purpose while Christ is for eternity. Look how John was described, 'John was a lamp that burned and gave light, and you chose for a time to enjoy his light' (John 5:35).

Two important principles may be derived from this verse. First, John was a lamp but he was not the Light (John 1:8). His little light emanated from the Light of the World. When all other bearers of light cease, when the sun, the stars and the moon darken, one Light will remain for eternity (Revelation 21:23) – Jesus! John declared: 'He must become greater; I must become less' (John 3:30).

Second, he knew that his mission was bound to end; his time was limited. He could waste no time; every opportunity was priceless. No matter how beautiful and shining his lamp was it would all come to an end.

Believers and fellow servants of God, we are not the Christ! No matter how important we think we are; no matter how bright our little light shines and people commend us, we have no right to receive the praise that belongs to God alone.

We are not the Christ, the Saviour of the world! The saved belong to Christ – his church, his bride. No matter how many souls we have brought to Christ let us remember that he is the bridegroom and, like John, we are the friends of the bridegroom who rejoice with him and then step back and become less.

One of the causes of downfall among ministers is pride garbed with identity crisis and miscalculation of time. There are those who act as if they were the Christ and their time on Earth is eternal. Ministers are never indispensable. The world needs Christ and our mission is to point them to Christ. Our time is limited. Therefore, we should fulfil our mission with urgency knowing that one day our time will be up and we will pass the baton to another.

John Wesley said: 'Do all the good you can, by all the means you can, in all the ways you can, in all the places you can, at all the times you can, to all the people you can, as long as you can.'

And if I may add, 'Give the glory back to God!'

The next important claim of John: '*I am* the voice' (John 1:23, Isaiah 40:3).

The voice of a person makes him or her distinct from other individuals. Through our voice, we express the deepest desires of our hearts. We speak our mind. We show our feelings. One sentence may be expressed with varying meanings according to the tone of voice.

A person may become the voice of another person as in the case of Moses and Aaron. At the start of Moses' mission he was timid and inarticulate. Aaron became his voice. Also, a person may become the voice of the majority, the spokesperson representing the people. John called himself the voice and alluded to Isaiah 40:3 as referring to him.

According to Strong's *Hebrew and Greek Bible Dictionary*, the word 'voice', as used in John 1:23, came from the word 'phone' (fo-nay) and gives the idea of disclosure, an address. This means that John, as the voice, is disclosing or revealing something. As the forerunner, he prepared the way for the coming of the Messiah – he was representing Christ.

In the Bible, the voice of God is represented in different ways. For Elijah, it was a still, small voice like a whisper in the wind (1 Kings 19:12-13) but for the Psalmist the voice of God resounded like a thunder (Psalm 18:13) and shook the desert (Psalm 29:8). It was a voice speaking out of fire for the Israelites (Deuteronomy 4:33). God chose how to express and reveal himself. The voices that he used were instruments of revelation.

In Malachi, God prophesied that he would send his messenger to prepare the way before him (Malachi 3:1). Therefore John, as the voice, was the messenger of God. Christ was the message and John was the messenger. The message was more important than the messenger. God chooses the messenger but the message remains the same! As the voice, John was crying, shouting and making a plea. The message was so important that he gave his all for it.

When God chooses a voice or a messenger, he expects the voice to represent him well by becoming faithful to the message. The voice must speak the mind of Christ, express the passion of Christ and live the life of Christ.

You and I are the voice of God! We proclaim the message that God is love and mercy so the world must see what love and mercy are according to God's principles. The world will accept or reject the message according to how they perceive the messenger.

SASB No 463 expresses the passion and prayer of a messenger:

Thou hast called me from the byway
To proclaim thy wondrous love;
Thou hast placed me on the highway
That to all men I may prove
There is mission in my living,
There is meaning in my word;
Saviour, in my daily striving
May this message yet be heard.

Chorus:
For thy mission make me holy,
For thy glory make me thine,
Sanctify each moment fully,
Fill my life with love divine.
   Brindley Boon

The next claim of John was '*I am* not worthy' (John 1:27).

I believe that the defining characteristic of humility is a maturing and never-changing sense of unworthiness. It is so easy to feel unworthy at the start of a ministry but as the person grows in knowledge and authority, the sense of unworthiness drifts away until pride takes over.

John said in Luke 3:16, 'But one who is more powerful than I will come, the straps of whose sandals I am not worthy to untie'. During biblical times, only the lowest slaves untied the sandals of their masters or visitors. In saying this, John did not only humble himself, he exalted Christ. If John, who was not a lowly slave, regarded himself as unworthy to untie the sandals of Christ, then who is worthy?

Usually, people feel unworthy because they compare themselves to other people. Discrimination based on gender, social status, race or physical appearance pushes many to the edge of the cliff of inferiority and self-pity. Surprisingly, even the rich and famous are not immune from the evil of self-pity and insecurity. On the contrary, true humility sets Christ as the standard for all comparison but, more than that, it sets Christ as the primary source of contentment and security. To recognise one's unworthiness before Christ is to acknowledge that only Christ can make us worthy. Before Christ, everyone is unworthy.

John declared that Christ's baptism was far greater than *his* baptism (Luke 3:16). John baptised with water; Christ will baptise with fire and the Holy Spirit. Christ's honour was far greater than his honour (John 1:27). Christ's leadership was supreme (John 1:35-41). Two of his disciples followed Jesus because of his declaration.

I would like to usher this message to an appeal for dedication or rededication. The words of Nathan C. Schaeffer are a challenge to all of us: 'At the close of life the question will not be how much have you got, but how much have you given; not how much have you won, but how much have you done; not how much have you saved, but how much have you sacrificed; how much have you loved and served, not how much were you honoured.'

Major Kelly Pontsler
USA Western Territory

To Tell the Truth
Psalm 24

DO you remember the American game show *To Tell the Truth*? It first aired on television back in 1956 and continued into the early 2000s. The show featured a panel of four celebrities attempting to correctly identify a contestant from a description. The contestant typically had an unusual occupation or had had an unusual experience. The 'real' person was joined by two others, imposters who pretended to be the real contestant.

To start every round, the three contestants would step out from behind a screen, all dressed alike and looking very much alike. The announcer would ask, 'What is your name, please?' Each challenger would say, 'My name is...' (inserting the name of the real contestant). The announcer would read a signed affidavit describing the real contestant and the contestants would have a seat. The panellists would then take turns asking questions, trying to figure out by the responses which contestant was the real one.

The imposters could answer just as they wanted and were allowed (even encouraged) to lie. The real contestant, though, was sworn to 'tell the truth'. At the end of the round, the panellists had to vote, identifying their choice of one, two, or three as the real contestant. Then the announcer would say, 'Will the real...please stand up?' and the studio audience would applaud with enthusiasm as the truth was revealed.

I remember watching the show as a young girl, making my guesses along with everyone else about who was the *real* contestant. Sometimes I got it right. Sometimes I got it wrong. It was amazing how persuasive

153

some contestants could be when they were telling outright lies! I'm not a good liar – are you? I do much better with telling the truth!

Truth and lies

I have been thinking about truth quite a lot recently. My session of cadets at The Salvation Army College for Officer Training was called Guardians of the Truth. What has been on my mind, though, has not been truth as a name of a game or as a title, but truth as an essential part of our Christian faith and walk; truth as a core element of who we are as committed Christians. Truth has been occupying my mind, along with the subject of integrity.

What does the word integrity mean to you? It comes from the same root as the word 'integer'. In maths, an integer is a whole number, such as one or two hundred and fifty-nine. It is never a fraction, like two-thirds. How much is one of something? How much is five-fifths of the same thing? In volume they are the same, but five-fifths tells us that the amount is subdivided, like an apple cut into pieces. The number one however is a complete unit, a whole number with no subdivisions, no fractions and no separate parts.

It is an important concept. Integrity – in the broadest sense of the word – is not just about honesty (telling the truth). Integrity means that there is wholeness. In common terms, it means that what I say, and what I think, and what I do all line up! There is a consistency. All that I am lines up, inside and out.

Being a person of integrity – authentic, consistent and real, the same through and through – is a high standard to reach, wouldn't you agree? Some time ago I did a personal exercise; to identify and write down my core values. I wrote down the things that are most important to me, those things I want to guide how I approach life. I've heard many seminar speakers talk about doing this, but had never really tried. So when I thought hard about it and then did the exercise, I realised that integrity was hugely important to me – right up there with my faith in God, having friends and family in my life, and keeping focused and purposeful.

154

Writing it down was a good start but a more important question was: do I live it out?

I can describe myself as being a particular way but does someone looking at me see the same thing? This is what I've been considering for some weeks now.

I think that at one time or another most of us are a bit like those 'imposter contestants'. We can look as good as the real thing, we can smile and give perfectly convincing answers, but when we get back to our room at night we know we're an imposter. We can blend in when we need to but in reality what shows on the outside is not who we are on the inside.

If we are really truthful, doesn't that describe most of us sometimes – even as Christians? We enjoy the fellowship of the congregation, we like hanging out with people who are positive and successful, and we want to be seen with the right crowd, hoping some of it rubs off! None of that is wrong but if we aren't careful we can let 'hanging out' with Christians replace actually becoming a Christ-follower ourselves. We can let reading books about the Bible replace actually reading and pondering the Bible. We can wear a uniform on the outside but have no heart connection to the soul-saving mission of our community of faith on the inside. Just spending time with clean people won't actually make us clean inside and out.

In Psalm 24 verses three and four (*NIV 1984*), David wrote: 'Who may ascend the hill of the Lord? Who may stand in his holy place? He who has clean hands and a pure heart...'

The Psalms were actually songs, and my study Bible says that these words were probably sung or spoken by a priest. These phrases are talking about who (what kind of person) can enter into the sanctuary and enter into worship.

We are told that God is holy through and through. So what kind of person is going to be ready to worship a holy God? Someone with clean hands (guiltless actions) and a pure heart (right motives). Someone whose inside matches the outside.

I don't think that David was saying that we have to be perfect to come to worship. Jesus himself spent time with people who society at large would have considered less than desirable friends – prostitutes, tax collectors, physically and emotionally disabled people, stubborn rugged fishermen who always opened their mouths without thinking! We certainly don't have to be perfect to have an encounter with the Lord.

But true worship, a deeper relationship with God our heavenly Father, our Creator, the one who plans our life, begins with clean hands and a pure heart. It begins when the inside and the outside line up.

Does that matter? What difference does it make? The writer of Proverbs says this: 'If you accept my words and store up my commands within you, turning your ear to wisdom and applying your heart to understanding, and if you call out for insight and cry aloud for understanding, and if you look for it as for silver and search for it as for hidden treasure, then you will understand the fear of the Lord and find the knowledge of God. For the Lord gives wisdom, and from his mouth come knowledge and understanding. He holds victory in store for the upright, he is a shield to those whose walk is blameless, for he guards the course of the just and protects the way of his faithful ones' (Proverbs 2:1-8 *NIV 1984*).

Let me repeat the last two verses; the Lord 'holds victory in store for the upright, he is a shield to those whose walk is blameless, for he guards the course of the just and protects the way of his faithful ones.'

'Victory for the upright' – to be upright is to be a person of integrity. 'A shield for the blameless' – sounds like clean hands to me. 'A guard for the just' – sounds like a pure heart to me, and that's where justice flows from. 'Protection for his faithful ones' – a life of integrity requires faithful attentiveness to how I live.

Who can enter into the deepest form of worship relationship with a holy God and stand in his holy presence? The one whose pure heart flows out in guiltless action. Who will God guard and protect in life? The one who remains faithfully pure in motive and blameless in action. This connection has certainly caught my attention!

Think about what kind of world you walk in, work in or raise a family in. I have realised afresh that walking with integrity in this world is hard to do. In the course of recent months I've seen good people accused of all sorts of things by people who lie. I've observed people saying one thing and doing another. I've read news stories about Christian people caught doing wrong things in places where they simply shouldn't have been.

How much we as Christians – as faithful followers of the Lord Jesus Christ – need to walk through this world as people of integrity. Integrity matters! Clean hands and pure hearts are essential. If we are going to influence others into a life of faith in the Lord Jesus Christ, then the inside and the outside must line up! It is possible, for God has promised victory, a shield, a guard, and protection for us.

Do you feel a need for victory in your life? Is something or someone making you feel you could use some protection? Are you walking right now through a minefield of temptation and desperately hoping to make it safely to the other side? Put the inside right – seek after and receive a clean heart. Let that clean heart flow out into the action you take on the outside; let it direct the way you live your life. Line it all up, be a person of integrity, and God will lead you to victory; he'll be your shield, your protection. As we allow the Holy Spirit to do his amazing work, to purify our hearts and mould our actions, our communion with God deepens. As that relationship grows, so does our capacity to live as God's people of integrity. That is what I truly want and need! How about you?

May God grant to us an ever-deepening understanding of his Word, and the courage to put it into action. Amen.

Captain Josephine Sabir Masih
Pakistan Territory

To Give to God

Genesis 4:1-7

Introduction

THE Scriptures tell us how we need to give to God. At the time of Harvest let us consider some of the stories about giving in the Bible so that we can think about them and learn about our own giving.

Genesis 4:1-7 tells the story of two brothers, Cain and Abel, who brought offerings to God. Cain's gift was not received in God's favour but Abel's was because it was the best animal that he had and a real sacrifice.

We have to be willing to deny ourselves; our giving to God needs to be sacrificial. We are meant to leave our personal preferences and to give instead to God. For example if I like biryani, I'll not eat biryani for a week, and give the money that I have saved by not eating my favourite curry dish to God.

The story of Hannah, found in 1 Samuel 2:18-21, helps us to understand sacrificial giving. From the story, we know that Hannah desperately wanted a child. Yet, when God finally blessed her with a precious son, she was willing to part with him and let him serve God in the temple. What a wonderful gift! She gave her son back to God and we know that God spoke to Samuel and used his life in a great way.

We also know about the story of Abraham and Isaac in the book of Genesis chapter 22. Abraham remained faithful to God and in return God gave him the gift of his son's life. Abraham had waited for this son, as his wife had been childless for many years, and he had a promise from God that his son would be the father of nations. Yet, when Abraham was called to sacrifice this dearly beloved precious child, he was willing to obey God and sacrifice him. Giving to God would have been costly for Abraham, but he obediently trusted God and because of this Isaac was spared.

In Mark 12:41-44 we read the story of the widow's offering. Jesus was in the Temple and he watched people give their offerings in the Temple. He saw wealthy people come and flamboyantly give from their riches, but the simple and humble giving of a poor widow moved Jesus. He was so stirred by this sacrificial giving that he called his disciples together and told them about it. The widow's giving had been truly sacrificial and Jesus valued it above the larger gifts of those who gave from their treasure store. Why? Because she was giving her food money – she was sacrificially giving all she had.

Ananias and Sapphira (Acts 5:1-11) is a tale of dishonesty in giving and the penalty paid for such behaviour. Everything they had sold belonged to them and the money received was theirs to keep or to give away. However, they chose to lie about their offering and give the impression that they were giving all that they had, much to their peril.

So we learn about how to give to God, by considering how not to give. Even if we have only a little to offer to God we need to give honestly to him.

Appeal

God gives us countless blessings – our children, homes, clothes, food, transport and so on. We should give thanks to him. The following Scripture references help direct our thoughts on giving the best that we have to God.

Exodus 23:19: 'Bring the best of the firstfruits of your soil to the house of the Lord your God.' God gives the promise that if we give in a way that honours God he will bless us abundantly. Proverbs 3:9-10: 'Honour the Lord with your wealth, with the firstfruits of all your crops; then your barns will be filled to overflowing, and your vats will brim over with new wine.'

We are also warned that, if we give sparingly or generously, so we will receive in return.

Mark 4:24: 'With the measure you use, it will be measured to you – and even more'.

If we give from our heart, God will reward our giving. Ananias and Sapphira's dishonesty in their giving to God resulted in their death, and the wealth of the world remained in this world. Abraham gave all and he was blessed in return. The widow gave generously from her meagre income and Jesus said she had given more than anyone else.

We have to give faithfully to God and here is an example of how we might do this: an appeal was going on in the church. Everyone had been invited to give more in the house of God. They were requested to bring what they wanted to give and put it in a large box at the front. A few women were seen putting their ornaments and jewellery in the box and others gave money. An elderly man in the congregation watched the proceedings and finally he came to bring his gift, but he was hardly able to walk. As he got to the box he put his walking stick aside and then sat inside the box.

Are our hearts like this? Do we want to give sacrificially? Do we give God our all?

We need to think about our giving to honour God.

Captain Japhette Sinda
Congo (Brazzaville) Territory

Our Thoughts are Contrary to Those of God

Jeremiah 45:1-5

A MESSAGE to Baruch:

'When Baruch son of Neriah wrote on a scroll the words Jeremiah the prophet dictated in the fourth year of Jehoiakim son of Josiah king of Judah, Jeremiah said this to Baruch: "This is what the Lord, the God of Israel, says to you, Baruch: You said, 'Woe to me! The Lord has added sorrow to my pain; I am worn out with groaning and find no rest.' But the Lord has told me to say to you, 'This is what the Lord says: I will overthrow what I have built and uproot what I have planted, throughout the Earth. Should you then seek great things for yourself? Do not seek them. For I will bring disaster on all people, declares the Lord, but wherever you go I will let you escape with your life.'"'

Introduction

God's mouthpiece, Jeremiah, invites us to direct our thoughts towards the reply that God gave to Baruch, son of Neriah. Let this reply deepen our spiritual understanding of the plan and will of God.

None of us likes suffering or sadness in this world. We all want to enjoy the good things of life in peace. Surely that is the ideal and the desire of everyone. But God's answer to Baruch shows us something quite different to what we expect of God in reply to our requests.

163

Pain and suffering

Verse three reveals Baruch's feelings. He was sad and discouraged in his sufferings. He found no rest and no response to his prayers. Tired and in despair, this servant of God wondered: 'The Lord has added sorrow to my pain'. Why? Because the Lord did not give him what he desired and he was constantly unhappy. He had asked great things from the Lord but God had not granted him what he wanted. God had another plan for the city – something that Baruch could not understand.

The Lord declares his intentions in verses four and five: 'I will overthrow what I have built and uproot what I have planted, throughout the Earth... I will bring disaster on all people... but wherever you go I will let you escape with your life.' So that is it! It was God's will to preserve the life of his servant, to protect him against evil and danger wherever he would go.

Many of us often complain about all sorts of things and, at times, we may feel unhappy and out of balance when the Lord does not solve our problems. Here are some questions that we may consider:

- Who among us knows the thoughts and desires of the Lord?
- Who among us is not discouraged when everything goes wrong?
- Who among us considers trials, attacks and suffering as God's will for us?

My dear brothers and sisters, here is the key message: God is faithful to his promises; he has an answer to our problems in one way or the other; among all the things we may ask of him in our prayers – marriage, children, health, prosperity – he will answer those prayers according to his will. He will do it!

So don't be discouraged, even if he does not act straight away because it is God, and God only, who knows your life and your future. Remember the answer that he gave to Baruch. And remember God's answer to Paul: 'My grace is sufficient' (2 Corinthians 12:9). If God did not meet the requests of Baruch, it is not because his ear was deaf or he would not listen.

It is not because his eyes were closed and he did not see Baruch's misery. No! But there were things to happen which Baruch knew nothing about – the destruction of the land and the coming disaster. For this reason God saw that he would gain nothing from his requests. Baruch's requests were inappropriate.

This is what we human beings do not always understand. People go to extremes, they prostitute themselves and they seek the help of the little gods of this world in order to obtain the answer to their prayers. Many have, in search of other powers, found only disaster and unhappiness.

My brothers and sisters in the Lord! God has a plan for each one. He is the one who knows our future. The plan he has for us is a plan of joy and not sorrow. He wants the best for us! Let us not be discouraged if the Lord does not give us what we have prayed for. Rather, let us ask that his will be done in us. The Bible tells us that 'a person's steps are directed by the Lord. How then can anyone understand their own way?' (Proverbs 20:24).

May God bless us all! Amen.

Major Kathryn Trim
Canada and Bermuda Territory

Make a Garden

Matthew 14:24-32

I LIKE to think in pictures. When I am learning something new, it helps me to make a picture in my mind of the information I am trying to learn. I use cookbooks with pictures of food, as I want to see what the end result will be. I prefer instruction books that are full of pictures and diagrams, as they help me really understand what I am supposed to do.

Many of us think in pictures. Have you ever attended a seminar or a workshop and heard the trainer say something like this: 'What do you want your future, your company, your church and your life to look like in five years time? Paint a picture in your mind. Create a vision. What do you see?'

A businesswoman may 'see' a company with offices spread across the country. A pastor may 'visualise' a church of 200 people worshipping and working together in unity. A mother may look ahead and 'picture' her children grown up, working in good jobs and with families of their own.

God gives us many pictures to help us understand his plan for our lives. The Bible is filled with them. Jesus taught in pictures all the time – his parables were 'picture' stories that helped people understand the truth. Think of the many visual ways in which Jesus described the Kingdom of Heaven. The Kingdom of Heaven is like:

- a mustard seed (Matthew 13:31)
- yeast (Matthew 13:33)
- a treasure hidden in a field (Matthew 13:44)

- a net let down into a lake (Matthew 13:47)
- a landowner who went out to hire workers (Matthew 20:1), and so on.

Each of these parables painted pictures and helped Jesus' listeners understand what he was teaching them.

I'd like to share one of my favourite Bible pictures. It is an image that helps us catch sight of what God can do in our lives. Let's explore the following verses and see what picture emerges.

'Blessed is the one who does not walk in step with the wicked or stand in the way that sinners take or sit in the company of mockers, but whose delight is in the law of the Lord, and who meditates on his law day and night. That person is like a tree planted by streams of water, which yields its fruit in season and whose leaf does not wither – whatever they do prospers' (Psalm 1:1-3).

'The Lord will guide you always; he will satisfy your needs in a sun-scorched land and will strengthen your frame. You will be like a well-watered garden, like a spring whose waters never fail' (Isaiah 58:11).

'The Lord will surely comfort Zion and will look with compassion on all her ruins; he will make her deserts like Eden, her wastelands like the garden of the Lord' (Isaiah 51:3).

So what's the picture? Yes, it's a garden! God wants to turn our lives into well-watered gardens. He plans to turn each of our children's lives into beautiful gardens. He wants us to be alive, to be beautiful and to bear fruit.

Let's think about what is involved in making a garden in our hearts. What does it take to transform us into places of beauty and fruitfulness?

Let's start with this fact: left on its own, a garden goes wild. Have you ever gone away for a long vacation and then come back to your property? Have you ever moved into a house where the previous owners were not gardeners? Have you left a plot of land unattended, even for only one season? What was it like?

Left unattended, nature goes wild. It is true of gardens and it is also true of people. It is true of our children.

When are you most likely to break the speed limit or cheat on your diet? When you know someone is watching or when you are all alone? When someone is policing your actions or when you are unattended? I have lived in places where the infrastructure of law and order has broken down and the result was not paradise, believe me; it was chaos!

Weeds seem to be stronger than cultivated plants. You don't have to teach a toddler to be selfish; it just comes naturally! No 'Garden of Eden' grows naturally in our hearts! Left to our own devices, we are a mess.

What does the Bible say? 'The heart is deceitful above all things...' (Jeremiah 17:9). 'For out of the heart come evil thoughts – murder, adultery, sexual immorality, theft, false testimony, slander' (Matthew 15:19). The 'back to nature', laissez-faire approach is disastrous both for gardens and human beings.

So now that we know what is not helpful for a garden, let us think about what is essential for a flourishing garden.

Plan

Nothing worthwhile in life 'just happens'! A good marriage, a strong business, a beautiful garden, a well-behaved child – anything done well is the result of good design and planning.

My favourite channel on television is [Canada's] HGTV. This is the channel that features house and garden shows. Many of the programmes feature makeovers with 'before and after' scenarios. A single room or an entire house is transformed before our eyes during the course of the programme.

The key figure in each transformation is the designer – someone who is able to look beyond the surface to create something wonderful and new. Each designer always has a plan. They know what the end result will look like and the changes that have to be made in order for that to take place.

What is true for homes and gardens is true for our lives. We need a good designer with a purpose and a plan for our transformation, because doing it in our own strength is virtually impossible.

The good news is that we have a designer for our lives! The greatest designer of all is our God. He wants to make a garden in your heart, and he knows exactly how to accomplish this. He is our master designer!

In Psalm 104:24 we read: 'How many are your works, Lord! In wisdom you made them all; the Earth is full of your creatures.' Our designer God has a plan for us. We read about this in Ephesians 1:11: 'In him we were chosen...according to the plan of him who works out everything in conformity with the purpose of his will.' This is reiterated in 2 Corinthians 3:18 *NIV 1984*, 'And we...are being transformed into his likeness', and Romans 8:29, 'For those God foreknew he also predestined to be conformed to the image of his Son...' God's plan is to transform our lives to be like Jesus. Jesus is our model of what God wants us to look and be like.

Will you admit that you need a designer with a plan for your life? Will you place your life into the hands of the Master Creator and allow him to renovate your heart? Will you take the time and effort to plan your family life? Will you make a commitment to God with respect to how you raise your children? Will you accept his plan for your children's lives, recognising that the most important thing for them is not that they know how to swim, or that they win first prize, or that they are the best dressed, or that they are the most popular, but that they grow up to be like Jesus?

Do you remember what Galatians 5:22 teaches us? '...the fruit of the Spirit is love.' What are the fruits of the Spirit that God wants to see growing in our lives and in the lives of our families?

To grow a great garden you must plan and plant.

Plant

So, you have a design. You know your land, the amount of light available, the quality of the soil and the length of the growing season. You have had to research and buy the foliage you plan to have in your garden. The next step is to prepare the beds and to plant/place them in the garden according to your plan. You position the shrubs, trees and flowers in the garden, many of which may not be indigenous.

God, the great designer, knows what needs to be planted in us. These are not things that grow in us naturally and because of this we need his help to become the beautiful gardens that the Bible talks about.

What does God plant in us?

- Life (Ephesians 2:4-5): 'But because of his great love for us, God...made us alive with Christ...'
- Himself (Philippians 2:13 *NIV 1984*): 'For it is God who works in you to will and to act according to his good purpose.'
- His Spirit (John 14:16-17 *NIV 1984*): '...I will ask the Father, and he will give you another Counsellor to be with you forever – the Spirit of truth...he lives with you and will be in you.' Romans 8:9: '...the Spirit of God lives in you.'
- His characteristics, to use gardening terms, his fruit (Galatians 5:22-23 *NIV 1984*): 'But the fruit of the Spirit is love, joy, peace, patience, kindness, goodness, faithfulness, gentleness and self-control.'

Sadly these are not characteristics which grow naturally within us. We need God, the great gardener, to plant and nurture these fruits in our lives. As God plants in us, so we must plant in our children. How will our children come to know Jesus? Only as we teach them! Society sends them a very pluralistic message in the school system. How will they learn the Scripture? Only as we read them biblical stories and encourage them to learn verses by heart! How will they bear fruit in their lives? Only as we plant good values into them and show them, by our example, how a true Christian behaves; as we demonstrate the fruit of the Spirit and reinforce those lessons which God is planting in their hearts and minds.

To create a garden you plan and plant, and then you feed.

Feed

What food does a garden require? A garden needs water, nutrients, and aerated soil. These are not the most glamorous components but are essential for every garden.

What do the gardens of our hearts require?

- Water (John 7:37 *NIV 1984*): 'Jesus…said…, "If anyone is thirsty, let him come to me and drink."' Coming to God and drinking is spending time in prayer with him.
- Nutrients (Matthew 4:4): 'Man shall not live on bread alone, but on every word that comes from the mouth of God.' The bread of life is the Bible, and we need to feed on God's words.
- Aerated soil: aeration is mixing up the soil in order to put air and water into it. It is done by literally putting holes in it. This prevents the soil from becoming too hard, too packed down and too difficult to work with.

We need to ask ourselves:

- What is feeding my life?
- What am I regularly putting into the garden of my heart?
- What is my nourishment?
- What do I read, watch and listen to?
- What is influencing my ideas and attitudes?

Is our heart more like a desert than a garden because it has been far too long since we watered it with prayer? Are we no longer producing any good fruit because we have stopped feeding our minds with God's word? Are we growing hard and stubborn because we are resisting the fellowship of others? We don't want other people to 'stab holes in our attitude' by challenging our ideas that might enable us to see things from a different perspective.

Good nutrition is essential for a thriving garden and family. In much the same way that our children need to eat well, so their hearts and minds need to be fed with good things. The Bible teaches us, '…whatever is true…noble…right…pure…lovely…admirable – if anything is excellent or praiseworthy – think about such things' (Philippians 4:8). Parents, please be very careful about what you feed your children, what you let into your homes on the television, the Internet and through your own choices. Remember, we are in the process of building beautiful gardens!

To make a garden you plan and plant, then you feed and, lastly, you weed.

Weed

Boy, oh boy, don't weeds spring up quickly? It seems as though they appear in the blink of an eye. There is no such thing as a once-and-for-all-time weeding. You have to keep pulling them out – practically every day! It takes continual diligence to remove them and keep them at bay.

Remember I said that you don't have to teach a toddler to be selfish, it just comes naturally? Sadly, all kinds of nasty things are inherent to our sinful nature. We have to be on guard against them, recognise them as soon as they try to establish themselves and pull them out!

The Bible warns us about these noxious weeds.

- Hebrews 12:15: 'See to it that...no bitter root grows up to cause trouble and defile many.'
- Ephesians 4:31: 'Get rid of all bitterness, rage and anger, brawling and slander, along with every form of malice.'
- Ephesians 4:29: 'Do not let any unwholesome talk come out of your mouths, but only what is helpful for building others up...'
- Ephesians 5:3: 'But among you there must not be even a hint of sexual immorality, or of any kind of impurity, or of greed, because these are improper for God's holy people.'
- Ephesians 5:18: 'Do not get drunk on wine, which leads to debauchery. Instead, be filled with the Spirit.'

The Bible is not one long list of regulations but rather guidelines on how to live because God knows human nature. Scripture gives us good advice about the things we need to rid our lives of, in order that we might be productive gardens.

Weeds spring up so quickly and can choke the life out of plants, so we need to build regular 'weeding' into our lives by studying God's word and taking it seriously. A helpful way to do this is to find an accountability partner – someone who knows you well and who will tell you honestly what they see. Give them permission, in fact beg them, to identify and pull out any weeds they see beginning to grow in your garden. Confession is good for the soul!

Make sure you pay attention to your children. Keep track of what is happening in their lives. Don't turn a blind eye to weeds or ignore troubling behaviour. Remember that you are their parent, not their best friend. Sometimes you will have to make unpopular decisions and they won't always like you, so be strong enough to stand up for what you know is right. Be fair, of course, and loving too. Ephesians 6:4: '...do not exasperate your children; instead, bring them up in the training and instruction of the Lord.'

But do not let weeds grow because it is such hard work to pull them out. Make the effort to be consistent in your discipline. Remember that you have to stay at it. Some days it will seem like the job is never done; that is because it isn't. The weeds are always ready to grow back. Be realistic and don't give up! With steady, constant care, a beautiful garden grows.

In summary: you plan, plant, feed and weed to achieve a beautiful garden. God's part is the planning and the planting (we give him permission and our co-operation). Our part is the feeding and the weeding. Yet, even in this, he is gracious and helps us when we cannot help ourselves.

In what condition is the garden of your heart? Is it still a wilderness? Have you not yet asked the great designer to take charge of your life? Have you accepted his plan to transform your life? If not, you have the opportunity to hand control of your wild heart to the great designer.

Is your heart a desert? Do you feel dry and lifeless and gasping for renewal? You haven't really watered your heart with prayer in a very long time. Have you forgotten to feed it? Does your Bible remain unopened on the bookshelf? Have you been trying to bear fruit without any nutrition? What kind of spiritual food are you feeding your children? Is it feast or famine for God's Word in your home?

Are weeds choking your life? Are you way too full of the nasty stuff that just seems to spring up naturally? Have you allowed bitterness, or a bad temper, or greed and impurity, to take root and grow in your heart. Have you resisted pulling out those thoughts, attitudes and habits that you know are bad for you?

The great designer is here and he has a good plan for your life. He wants to transform you into something amazing. He can plant new life, his Sprit, his Word and his character into your life. Will you let him? Pray these words of the psalmist: 'Create in me a clean heart, O God; and renew a right spirit within me' (Psalm 51:10 *KJV*).

Be confident that, 'The Lord will guide you always; he will satisfy your needs in a sun-scorched land and will strengthen your frame. You will be like a well-watered garden, like a spring whose waters never fail' (Isaiah 58:11).

Major Marieke Venter
Southern Africa Territory

Citizens of Heaven

Genesis 4:3-9, Philippians 3:20, Luke 4:18-19

Introduction

THERE was a brave man who spent his days on the banks of a powerful, surging river. People would often fall into the raging waters from the rickety bridge that crossed the river, and he had made it his life's task to rescue them. Though he saved many lives, some still drowned.

One day a visitor asked him: 'Why do you spend so much time rescuing people? Would it not be better to spend time fixing the bridge, making it strong and secure? That way, people wouldn't fall into the river, and lives would be saved.'

The Church, and especially The Salvation Army, spends a lot of time rescuing people. We rescue them from the streets. We rescue them from the hands of abusers. We rescue them from abandonment. We rescue them from hunger and poverty. We rescue them from homelessness. And it's a wonderful ministry we have. It is a work we undertake with love and compassion, in the name of Jesus. We must never stop rescuing people.

Today we are challenged with the same questions the man at the river faced: is there not a way to mend the bridge? Is there not a way to prevent some of the casualties we rescue day after day? Is there perhaps a way to build a society that does not have so many tragedies? A society where people are not crippled by poverty, suffering and injustice?

Some Christians would answer these questions by saying that we should focus only on spiritual things, like prayer and preaching and

177

evangelism. After all, they may say, we are citizens of Heaven. And we should not waste time getting involved in 'worldly' issues like poverty, hunger, abuse, disease and injustice!

This leads us to another question, and I think it's an important one, well worth exploring: 'How do citizens of Heaven live while they are on Earth?'

Of course, Heaven did send its number one citizen to Earth for a while, so maybe we can take a brief look at how he, Jesus – Crown Prince of Heaven – spent his time while he was on Earth. We could assume that he spent all his time conducting prayer meetings, evangelical campaigns and discipleship seminars. Well, he did all those, but if we read the gospels carefully we find that he did much more than that. He got involved in the lives of the people, he cared about their circumstances, their families, their struggles to survive, their hunger and their needs.

So how do citizens of Heaven live while they are on Earth?

Citizens of Heaven take responsibility on Earth

Our problem with taking responsibility started centuries ago, right in the first book of the Bible. Genesis 4:3-9 tells the story of two brothers, Cain and Abel. Cain murdered his brother Abel. God asked Cain about his brother, and his answer to that question still echoes around the world, 'Am I my brother's keeper?' (v 9).

Am I called upon to care if my fellow human being is hungry, or abused, or enslaved? Am I expected to take responsibility when people in my community suffer from poverty and unemployment? God's word says we are – Christ's life says a resounding yes – and he proved it on Calvary.

'My God, my God, why have you forsaken me?'(Matthew 27:46) was his cry as he hung dying on the cross. Why indeed? Because Christ had taken responsibility by taking the sins of the world upon himself. In the words of Philippians 2:7-8, he '...taking the very nature of a servant...becoming obedient to death', became sin for the sake of a lost humanity. Jesus took responsibility regardless of the personal cost.

Citizens of Heaven take action on Earth

Major Campbell Roberts said the following: 'We who have received complete love from Christ are called to give transparent witness to justice, peace, equality and holiness through actions which redeem and re-order the world.'

Redeem and re-order? Listen to the words of Christ as he defines his mission in Luke 4:18-19: 'The Spirit of the Lord is on me, because he has anointed me to proclaim good news to the poor. He has sent me to proclaim freedom for the prisoners and recovery of sight for the blind, to set the oppressed free, to proclaim the year of the Lord's favour.'

It sounds like a complete turnaround of the existing social order of the day! If you continue to read Luke 4, you will find that his words spark quite a debate, and it all ends with an attempt on his life in verse 29 as they try to push him off a cliff! Citizens of Heaven take action and are not afraid of opposition or even danger.

The important people groups in Jesus' mission statement were the poor, the prisoners, the blind and the oppressed. William Booth cared about the same people, and his passion gave birth to The Salvation Army. We were raised to serve the poor, the prisoners, the blind and the oppressed – are we still serving them today?

Steve Chalke talks about taking social action in his book *Intelligent Church*. He writes: 'Wherever real needs exist, the church has a God-given, Christ-inspired mandate to be engaged. Asylum, poverty, people-trafficking, housing, education, employment, health care, youth issues, crime, marriage, community development, the environment, regeneration, trade justice, globalisation, human rights, addiction, discrimination…are just a few areas where real needs exist.'

Why should we take social action? Why should we show practical love by helping to create a better society? Because that's what Christ did for us! He did not remain in the glorious golden streets of Heaven. He came to our world and lay helplessly in the rough hands of a carpenter and in the clumsy arms of a young mother. Jesus came and walked on the dusty roads of Earth and he got involved in the lives of the people, the widows, the tax collectors, the sinners, the prostitutes and the

179

children. He spoke about reordering society and making a world that would be fair and just in which the poor might have enough, where the blind might see, where the oppressed and the unjustly imprisoned would be free.

Citizens of Heaven take a stand on Earth

Perhaps by this time you are thinking: 'I would love to help and get involved in creating this world that Christ spoke about. But that world will never be! That world will be waiting for us in Heaven, but it is not attainable down here.'

That may be true. But until we take up our permanent residence in Heaven, we are also citizens of Earth. We are our brothers' keepers. We are called upon to take responsibility, to take action, and to take a stand.

In our country, election talk is being heard. Debates are the order of the day on the radio stations and television programmes. Party political manifestos are being proclaimed in the hope of persuading voters to elect their party into government.

The people of South Africa will go to the polls and cast their vote, and at the end of the democratic process a result will be revealed and we will say: 'The people have spoken!'

Brothers and sisters, we have a voice. It may be a small voice, and it may seem insignificant but we need to exercise our right to vote. Maybe some people will say to themselves: 'Christians shouldn't get mixed up in politics. Christians shouldn't vote. Salvationists shouldn't vote!' Imagine for a moment if all the Christians did not vote on voting day. If we all stayed home, the people who don't know God, who don't have godly guidance in their choices, who don't have God's word to apply to the issues of the day, would choose who governs our country.

Citizens of Heaven, we must speak out on Earth. Christ did! When he defended the woman who was about to be stoned, when the disciples tried to chase away the children who were brought to him, when they criticised the woman who anointed him generously with expensive perfume, he took a stand.

180

Application

We have prayed over the last weeks for the people in Zimbabwe and in the Middle East, for peace and justice. Perhaps we can do no more than pray for people in other parts of the world. But here in our own country, we have a voice! Let us take the next step – take responsibility, take action and take a stand. The least we can do is to make our voice heard. Not mindlessly, but having researched which party will rule with wisdom and justice. Having carefully listened to the political manifestos, prayed about our choice sincerely, consulted the Scriptures thoroughly and sought God's wisdom. Now comes the responsibility to cast your vote, as citizens of Heaven who live in the world and care for it, because our God loves the world.

The thought that we are citizens of Heaven gives us great comfort. It assures us that our reward will be in Heaven. It promises us a future and a hope. We look forward with keen anticipation to the day when all things will be made new, and we enter those golden gates and walk along those golden streets!

But in the meantime, until we enter our 'real' homeland, God calls us to be good citizens of our current, temporary home on Earth. We must take responsibility on Earth, we must take action on Earth, and we must take a stand on Earth.

Major Sabrina Williams
Caribbean Territory

Prayer, our Daily Food

John chapter 17

JESUS not only taught his disciples the importance of prayer, but he also modelled it in his daily life. As believers, we need this vital source of nutrition for our spiritual growth and development.

Let us look at three aspects of prayer.

Prayer – a God-given priority

While many believers sincerely desire to spend time with God in prayer, the reality is that few actually do. Spiritual discipline is necessary to make prayer a priority in our lives. God has made prayer a priority, directing his children to pray first, often and at all times. Prayer should therefore become a priority for us.

Scripture speaks repeatedly of the importance of prayer. Paul instructs us to pray about everything (Philippians 4:6). Believers should make all requests known to God. In addition, believers are admonished to pray regularly and frequently. King David promised the Lord, 'Morning, noon, and night I cry out in my distress, and the Lord hears my voice' (Psalm 55:17 *NLT*). Jesus prayed for extended periods of time, especially when making important decisions (Luke 6:12).

When facing challenges or trials, it is natural for us to pray (James 5:13). Paul exhorted the Christians in Thessalonica to pray without ceasing (1 Thessalonians 5:17). Prayer should become not only an attitude of the heart but also a continual dialogue with the Lord.

When praying, take time to be still and hear a word from God (Psalm 46:10). The Bible dictates no specific time or place for prayer. However, a believer may find it easier to maintain the priority of prayer when they establish a definite time and place to pray as part of their daily schedule.

Prayer should occupy a place in the heart and it also needs a place in the home. While every believer does not need a prayer closet as specified in Matthew 6:6, all believers need to have a place of solitude free from distraction in order to pray in private.

Prayer – a God-given purpose

Prayer is the opportunity God gives to his children to become intimately acquainted with him. It is helpful to see prayer as a conversation with God, enabling the believer to build a personal relationship with him. Prayer is an expression of a believer's dependence on God and, at the same time, an affirmation of God's promise to the redeemed for spiritual power.

The primary purpose of prayer is to seek God's will. Jesus, in his model prayer, told his disciples to ask according to the will of God (Matthew 6:10). When a believer talks to their heavenly Father, each request for help and guidance should be made in the name of Jesus. All of the conditions related to prayer are bound up in this phrase 'according to his will'.

Prayer provides an opportunity for adoration, praise, thanksgiving, confession of sin and intercessory prayer. Numerous formats for prayer are possible; in fact, prayer is unique to each person, but all prayer has a central purpose of expressing oneself fully and honestly to the Lord, to listen for his reply (very often in the form of insight, assurance and joy) and to participate in the 'mystery' of seeing God's purposes accomplished.

Prayer also offers an opportunity for Christian fellowship and guidance for the church. Prayer is not intended as a means of impressing others or manipulating God but as a way of genuinely seeking God's strength and direction.

Prayer – a God-given provision

Many Christians have needs that are not met, simply because they do not pray (James 4:2). While God does not promise to provide all we want, he does provide all we need (Philippians 4:19). He is our all-sufficient provider.

Prayers for provision are generally expressed in one of two ways: personal petitions or intercession. Personal petitions are the requests a believer makes for their own needs. Intercessions are prayers for the needs of others. Even when the believer does not know how to pray, the Holy Spirit intercedes on the believer's behalf (Romans 8:26-27).

While the model prayer Jesus gave includes only a request for daily bread (Matthew 6:11), Jesus introduced that prayer to his followers by telling them to 'ask him' for whatever they needed (Matthew 6:8). God promises to provide for the needs of his children. He provides for their physical needs for food, clothing and shelter. He provides for their spiritual needs through prayer, Bible study, and various forms of ministry in his name. God will provide for his children as they seek his help through prayer.

Fellow believers, let us feed daily on this important food so that we can mature and grow, becoming more and more like Jesus.

God richly bless you.

Major Morag Yoder
USA Central Territory

I Know He Watches Me

Genesis chapter 16, Psalm 121, Matthew 10:29-31

AT the back of my study Bible there is a comprehensive section of Bible helps, including character studies. Biographical sketches for many of history's prominent men are right at my fingertips – but, strangely, no women are included.

Some men and women of the Bible come to life because they are pivotal characters in stories of intrigue and drama, while others are noteworthy only because their names are so difficult to pronounce. For example, when reading chapters 15-18 of Genesis, Abraham and Sarah loom larger than life in a tale of epic proportions. God chose them and spoke directly to them with mind-boggling promises, yet every encounter they have with God seems to leave them grappling with unanswered questions and struggling to believe. Sometimes I love their oh-so-human reactions, while at other times my contemporary mind cringes at the outrageousness of their actions. Right from the start this Old Testament husband and wife duo command centre stage.

Woven into the story of this couple is the tale of one of history's 'little people', the seemingly insignificant Hagar. We don't know for certain when Hagar entered the picture, but we do know she appears as a vulnerable, disregarded, abused and messy complication in a major Old Testament account. Hagar's name isn't included in any of the character lists in my Bible, but Scripture teaches us that this woman registered with God.

187

Listen to what Frederick Douglass, abolitionist and former American slave, wrote in his book *My Bondage and My Freedom*: 'What an assemblage! Men and women, young and old, married and single; moral and intellectual beings, in open contempt of their humanity, level at a blow with horses, sheep, horned cattle, and swine! Horses and men, cattle and women, pigs and children – all holding the same rank in the scale of social existence, and all subjected to the same narrow inspection, to ascertain their value in gold and silver – the only standard of worth applied by slaveholders to their slaves!'

Hagar, an African slave, might have entered the Genesis story in chapter 12 when Abram entered Egypt and coaxed his wife into pretending to be his sister. This scam resulted in a serious situation with the Pharaoh. Abram was sent out of Egypt, but in the process he became a rich man. Hagar might have been a gift from Pharaoh – given along with livestock, gold and silver.

Genesis chapter 16 *NIV 1984* opens with this straightforward reference, 'Sarai, Abram's wife…had an Egyptian maidservant named Hagar'. Eyes easily skim over the words. No emotion is tied to Hagar's name, or occupation. She's hardly worth mentioning, barely visible – but let the truth of the sentence sink in.

Hagar; a person, a human being, a woman trapped in slavery. No rights, no dignity, wrong gender, wrong race, dehumanised, powerless, cut off from family, her country, her history. She was a common slave – given to serve – a piece of property. There was no one to look out for her, no one to care for her, no one to protect her, no belongings of her own, not even the right to her own body.

Are there invisible people on the sidelines of your life story or mine? If someone wrote down my day-to-day history, would I be surprised to find people included who are invisible to me? Or maybe you are the one who feels invisible, overlooked, unrecognised?

Sarai and Abram, our aged main characters, seem to be struggling to understand how God will fulfil his promise to make their descendants as numerous as the stars in the sky. Hagar is mentioned only because Sarai decides that perhaps God isn't able to keep his promise. She takes matters into her own hands by concocting a plan to assist him.

By law and custom, Sarai did nothing wrong, but it's important to note that God may reject social customs. Just because everyone is doing it doesn't make it right! Given the context of time and place, Sarai's actions might not have been unusual but, nevertheless, I would expect Hagar was left feeling hurt and abused by the process.

Verses two to four sound strange and uncomfortable to my modern-day ears. Some scholars have compared these verses to Genesis 3:6; the account of Eve 'taking' the fruit and 'giving' it to Adam. Sarai 'took' Hagar and 'gave' her to Abram. Invisible Hagar had no rights, no voice, no meaning. She seems to be simply a way for Abram and Sarai to get what they wanted.

With this action, the plan Sarai initiates is set in motion. Abram agrees, Hagar submits. The plan succeeds – or does it? Hagar becomes pregnant, but she certainly doesn't seem thrilled with the prospect of surrogate motherhood. In fact, we read in verse five that she began to despise her mistress. The plan adds insult to injury, and Hagar can no longer hide her feelings. She loathes the woman she serves; she hates being used in this most intimate and demeaning way. She bristles with rage at the injustice. Discovering she is vital to what Sarai most wants empowers Hagar to openly display her scorn and the plan turns sour.

How does Sarai react? Shock or rage? She is incensed by Hagar's insolence. First, she selfishly and childishly whines and complains to her husband, but all he does is shrug his shoulders. It's as if neither woman matters to him. He has a household on the verge of explosion and, instead of trying to diffuse the situation or bring about some truce, he takes the easy way out. I can only think Abram's lack of response added fuel to his wife's fire! And Sarai's fire becomes another stain on this family's story when she mistreats Hagar.

But what's the big deal? Hagar is a slave, a piece of property. She's a nobody. 'Mistreat' isn't such a horrible-sounding word, is it? But this same word, as used in the *Contemporary English Version* of Exodus 1:11-12, describes Egypt's oppression of the Israelites. To be in Egyptian bondage was like being in a furnace strong enough to melt iron. The word 'mistreated' as used here means ruthless treatment. Sarai unleashes her fury on her pregnant servant!

How could this have happened within one of history's most significant households of faith? Sadly, the actions and choices made in this brief account lead to trouble that plagues Abraham and his descendants. Now the plot twists, the turning point comes, and suddenly Hagar moves from the sidelines of the story to centre stage. As a result of Sarai's actions, Hagar runs away. This pregnant, vulnerable, humiliated, frightened woman – this invisible character – steps into the spotlight and introduces us to a powerful aspect of God.

Just when Hagar feels abandoned and most afraid, a huge search and rescue beam (just like one of those amazing spotlights that scan the night sky) falls on her. Hagar, unseen for much of her life, becomes the focal point and discovers she is a woman of value, dignity and purpose. Verse seven of Genesis chapter 16 tells us 'The angel of the Lord found Hagar'. God didn't stumble across her. This was no chance encounter. Hagar was sought and found! She registered on God's radar all along.

We can assume that Hagar had heard about the God of Abraham – the God of Heaven and Earth, the great Jehovah – while serving her mistress. Do you think she ever wondered if this all-powerful God truly existed? Now, at the moment when she feels most alone, she is caught off guard by the presence of God himself. He doesn't come as a great, awesome, far-off mystery; he comes with understanding, as a personal, intimate reality. God intervenes in Hagar's life. (Some commentators say that this Old Testament angel of the Lord is the pre-incarnate Jesus – the same Jesus, our Saviour, who demonstrates to all mankind that we are not invisible to God.) God knew all about Hagar, and, for the first time in the story, she is addressed by name, proving that she matters to God.

King's Cross train station is in a rather notorious area of London and for a year I travelled in and out of it while taking a university course. It was one of the stations hit during the 7/7 London bombings, but it is probably best known because it sits in London's red light district. King's Cross heaves with humanity every minute of every day, yet it is home to some of life's most 'invisible' people.

I discovered that right in the middle of this community, sitting like a beacon of hope, is The Salvation Army's Faith House. Two officers, Majors Estelle Blake and Christine Kingscott, manage the house and move about the community like angels of mercy; working with prostitutes, drug addicts, illegal immigrants, sex traffickers and the mentally ill. People who, for a variety of reasons, ran away from their previous lives, and now live in fear and vulnerability. Almost every night these two women walk the area. They look for new faces, check on regulars and stop to talk to everyone. Chris and Estelle never pass anyone by. No one is invisible to them. Why do they do this? It's because they carry God's message that every human being is valuable to God. No one is more important than those who feel lost and invisible.

Hagar's story is rich in meaning. The awesome God of Israel reveals that his eye is fixed on an individual. Hagar moves from being invisible, to being sought and found, to becoming the *visible* woman. God's purposes are always redemptive, and this encounter gives us a clear indication that God cares for all people. His plan includes non-Jews, slaves and even women. We read in Galatians 3:28, 'you are all one in Christ Jesus', but to those living in Old Testament times this news was extraordinary.

Hagar is changed and empowered by this encounter. So confident is she, this 'nobody' dares to give God a name. She calls him 'El Roi,' – 'the God who sees me'. Hagar provides us with a basic truth – so pure, so uncomplicated – a truth we can't afford to miss. Hagar wasn't invisible to God, and this truth gives her courage to act in freedom. Maybe for the first time she chooses obedience instead of being forced to comply. She does what God asks of her and returns to her mistress. Hagar takes her new faith to the place she most fears: to the people who mistreated her.

I think back to early lessons I received about God: omnipotence (unlimited power), omnipresence (present in all places at all times) and omniscience (infinite awareness, understanding and insight). Big words for a big God! Yet, as a child, these strange-sounding words made God seem

191

all the more far away. It's like telling me something is worth a trillion dollars. I can't grasp that amount – a number like that is too huge. I'll never see or have that much money, so it's impossible for me to fully comprehend what that amount of money means.

Hagar's story makes the concept of God's omniscience completely understandable and personal. Hagar's story tells me that God sees us, not just with his eyes, but with his heart.

Maybe I've been too rough on Abram and Sarai. This Scripture helps me understand that both Sarai and Hagar needed to learn the same lesson about God. They both felt alone and forgotten, believing no one understood the difficulty of their life's experience. Each woman needed to know she mattered to God.

Do you ever feel invisible? Are you afraid? Do you think that God has lost sight of you? You are not invisible to God! The Bible tells us that God is so intimately involved in our lives he knows the exact number of hairs on our heads. No one else knows that much detail about me!

None of us lives free from hardship, and yet like Hagar we are each called to respond to God in faith. Running away when things are tough isn't the answer. We only take our problems with us and often discover we've now created new ones. Faith means we trust God's Word and wait patiently for the fulfilment of his promises. When the waiting leads to distress, we rest in the certainty that God sees, hears and understands. Hagar's encounter with 'the God who sees' changed the way she viewed her circumstances.

Sometimes people (both men and women) feel invisible, abandoned, lost, alone and forgotten because of age, bereavement, disability, illness, marital status, a history of abuse, or family circumstances. Maybe you've given up on waiting for any good to come from your pain. Maybe you've taken matters into your own hands instead of waiting on God's intervention. Do you think he doesn't see you?

To sense God's presence perhaps you simply need to stop moving long enough for his rescue beam to fall upon you. Stop running. Stop trying to fix things on your own. Right here, right now, in this very moment, at this very spot. This is the place where God wants to meet with you.

Matthew 10:29-31 says, 'Are not two sparrows sold for a penny? Yet not one of them will fall to the ground outside your Father's care. And even the very hairs of your head are all numbered. So don't be afraid; you are worth more than many sparrows.'

God sees you. He knows. You matter. You are not invisible. He knows your name. Will you dare to believe?

Lieut-Colonel Rebecca Yousaf
Pakistan Territory

Forward with Prayer

Philippians 4:4-7

Introduction

THE theme of our territory in 2010 was 'Forward with Prayer'. When we pray we make requests, we offer thanksgiving and listen to God and remind ourselves of all that he is.

If we are going forward with prayer, we need to take others with us – elders, youth, boys, girls, men and women. We also want to take our family forward with prayer. This includes our relatives who don't trust God, idol worshippers, the sick, childless couples and the needy. It is important to pray for one another and to confess our own sins.

Let us see from the Bible how people move forward in trying times through the power of prayer. We will see their obedience to God and their strength of faith.

Hannah's prayer
1 Samuel 1:10-11

Hannah was childless and, as in a culture like ours in Pakistan, it meant that she was ridiculed and was a disappointment to her family. This is never easy for any woman, but Hannah turned her thoughts to God. We know that God answered her prayers and she gave her son to the temple as she had promised.

Allow me to share a story with you. In *Nara-e-Jang* [*The War Cry* of Pakistan] the Women's Ministries Department report from Islamabad featured the story of a woman who was unable to have children. She went to the captain of the local corps and asked the officer to pray for her. The officer agreed to pray, but she also invited her to come to the Army so that she could start to pray regularly with her about having a child. The lady began to attend the corps and now after 10 years she is expecting her first child.

Esther's prayer
Esther 4:15-16
Esther and her people were in a perilous situation. Esther seemed to be the only possible solution. She asked her people to fast and pray for her and then she prepared to break court protocol – a dangerous act – and approach the king without invitation. She carefully prepared herself, bathed herself, dressed her hair and put on her most exquisite gown. Most importantly, she prepared herself in prayer. She knew that she may have died for this action, but she moved 'forward' with prayer and saved her nation.

Daniel in the lions' den
Daniel chapter 6
King Darius ordered that no one should bow before any god but himself. Daniel, a Jew, had a disciplined prayer life, he believed in the one true God and he was not prepared to break the commandment found in Exodus 20:3, 'You shall have no other gods before me'. He was not going to change his practice and so he continued to pray three times a day. This is discovered and reported to King Darius who then sentenced him to death by being thrown into the lions' den. Daniel knew this was a possibility but he was brave and faithful and worshipped only God. So when he was thrown into the den God protected him and his life was spared.

To go forward sometimes requires courage and faithful obedience to God's will. Daniel not only continued to believe in God but also, because of his witness, the king and all people of the nation bowed before God.

Paul and Silas
Acts 16:25-31

If you found yourself in prison, with your feet and hands in the stocks, I am sure you wouldn't want to sing. In the story of Paul and Silas, they found themselves in a tricky situation where they were unfairly treated, bound and tortured. Instead of questioning God and lamenting their situation they chose to pray and sing hymns of praise to God. God rewarded their faith and they were freed from their bonds but they stayed in their prison cell.

This strong witness influenced the jailer and we learn that the way forward from the prayers of Paul and Silas was that the jailer and his family believed. Moving forward with prayer may mean moving on through difficult circumstances and trusting God for release.

A Pharisee and tax collector
Luke 18:9-14

Jesus uses a Pharisee and a tax collector to teach us how we should pray. The Pharisee is a proud man and arrogant in his prayers, so his prayers are not acceptable to the Lord. The tax collector, however, is humble and he approaches his prayers by admitting he is not fit for the presence of God.

We can learn from this in our prayer lives, as we desire to move forward with God. It cannot be for our own glory but rather to bring glory and honour to the name of Jesus. God has the power to bring about change in our lives as a result of our sincere and fervent prayers.

Elijah's prayer
1 Kings 18:41-46

James refers to the effectiveness of Elijah's prayers (James 5:16-18). Would we be ready to stand in front of crowds of people and pray for no rain and then years later to do the same, this time asking for rain? Would we expect God to honour those prayers?

What a witness these prayers were! This passage has relevance not only for Elijah but also for our churches today. Elijah was an ordinary person like you and me, and he prayed fervently, believing that God would answer his prayer. God used his miracle-working power – he often uses his servants to demonstrate his power – and answered Elijah's prayer. God could be planning to use one of us to announce a miracle, so he can display his power and glory.

Hezekiah's prayer
2 Kings 20:1-6
Hezekiah was on the point of death. The prophet Isaiah went to him and told him to make arrangements for himself as he was going to die. Hezekiah turned his face towards the wall and prayed to God: 'Remember, Lord, how I have walked before you faithfully and with wholehearted devotion and have done what is good in your eyes' (v 3). God answered his prayer and said: '…I have heard your prayer and seen your tears; I will heal you…I will add 15 years to your life' (vv 5-6).

Jesus' prayer
Mark 14:32-36
Prayer was important in the life of Jesus. We read about Jesus going apart from others so that he could pray. We read his prayers in Scripture (John chapter 17) and in this passage he gives us instruction on how to pray.

He wants us to separate ourselves to spend time in prayer with him so that he is the focus of our prayers. He also invites us to pray so that we do not fall into temptation.

Application
We want to move forward, but not in our own direction or in our own strength. We want to move forward in the direction and ways that God ordains for each one of us. In order to do this we need to depend on his strength and grace.

As we think about these Bible characters and their prayer stories, we are challenged to think about what God is saying to us:

- Do I want to move forward or am I content to stay the way I am?
- Can I trust God enough for me to take a courageous step forward?
- What does 'forward' mean in my life?
- How do I know what God is asking me to do?

Available June 2012

From Her Heart – Selections from the Preaching and Teaching of Helen Clifton

Chosen by General Shaw Clifton (Retired), this compilation represents writings from almost every phase of Commissioner Helen Clifton's influential service as a Salvation Army officer – including testimonies, personal insights from her prayer diaries, and material from her time as World President of Women's Ministries.

Love – Right at the Heart
Robert Street

Written in harmony with General Linda Bond's call – One Army, One Mission, One Message – this book examines how Christians have a responsibility to one another, whilst taking their caring ministry to the world. Through Sam and Joe's informal 'After the meeting' sessions and a subsequent 'Heart to heart' section, each aspect of love is considered in the context of day-to-day service.

144pp (paperback), illustrations, sheet music, link to mp3 download
ISBN 978-0-85412-841-9

Can be purchased from any Salvation Army trade or supplies department and online at www.amazon.co.uk

Essentials of Christian Experience –
Classic Salvationist Text
Frederick Coutts

Originally published in 1969, this
book permits the 21st century
reader an insight into the thoughts
which General Coutts shared with
many thousands of people in a
variety of locations and situations
during the time of his ministry.

128pp (paperback)
ISBN 978-0-85412-838-9

Other titles in the *Classic Salvationist Texts* series include:
Purity of Heart – William Booth
Practical Religion – Catherine Booth
The Desert Road to Glory – Clarence Wiseman

**Can be purchased from any Salvation Army trade
or supplies department and online at
www.amazon.co.uk**

Army on its Knees

Janet Munn and Stephen Court

To equip you to win the world for Jesus, this book describes the fundamentals of prayer – from private prayer to missional prayer. In these pages the writers inspire readers to deploy the power of prayer in the battle that has eternal consequences for the realisation of the Great Commission.

Army on its Knees is both an exciting testimony to the power of prayer, and a call to arms for this generation.
Pete Greig, Co-founder, 24-7 Prayer and Director of Prayer, Alpha International

136pp (paperback), illustrations
ISBN 978-0-85412-842-6

Can be purchased from any Salvation Army trade or supplies department and online at www.amazon.co.uk